PRAYING
EFFECTUALLY

Praying Based on God's Word

REV. MACARTHUR EDMUNDSON, TH.D.

authorHOUSE®

AuthorHouse™
1663 Liberty Drive
Bloomington, IN 47403
www.authorhouse.com
Phone: 833-262-8899

Published by AuthorHouse 03/22/2021

ISBN: 978-1-6655-2068-3 (sc)
ISBN: 978-1-6655-2067-6 (e)

Library of Congress Control Number: 2021905927

Print information available on the last page.

Any people depicted in stock imagery provided by Getty Images are models, and such images are being used for illustrative purposes only. Certain stock imagery © *Getty Images.*

This book is printed on acid-free paper.

All scriptures were taken from the King James Version of the Bible.

CONTENTS

INTRODUCTION

From the very beginning, God mandated that He be put first in the lives of His people. No individual can lay claim to being in the right relationship with God without first adhering to a relationship that places God above self. It is not for reasons of selfishness, greatness, or smallness that God demands to be put first in the life of believers – instead, it is quite the opposite. Should God choose not to require that He be first in our lives – He would relinquish His position as sovereign, which would contradict Him being God. Since Man is human, he needs God's rulership over him. Our life comes from God; therefore, without Him, man cannot exist. Moreover, in rebellion against God's rule, Man rushes toward his misery and destruction in sinful activities and by false idols. Placing God first is not just something that a Christian should do, nor is it just some admirable goal or high ideal that is unattainable in the practical sense. On the contrary, putting God first is the primary mandate of the divine laws of the kingdom of God.

Every sincere child of God desires to pray effectually. We want our prayers to be heard by Him and acted upon favorably. We can pray effectually – we can know that our prayers will reach God and that He will act upon them. God is no respecter of persons – He loves every one of us the same. He will hear one person's prayers as quickly as another when we meet the condition required for effective praying. God has not left us in the dark regarding a subject as vital as prayer. He has given us principles and requirements so that we can pray effectually. He desires to answer our prayers and has given us a definite direction for worship. Perhaps no other virtue demonstrates genuine Christ-like as much as does forgiveness. Christians are given a lot of attention for Charity acts, for energetic worship,

and for maintaining the moral quality of a spiritual setting. But a Christian who will not forgive is like salt that has lost its savor – he is fit for nothing.

Prayer is one of the highest privileges for the children of God. In some instances, it is one of the most neglected weapons in our arsenal by which we war against the flesh and the devil. The Lord Jesus Christ highly recommends that "Men ought always to pray, and not faint" (Luke 18:1). The Christian's love for prayer, the Word of God, and the experience of the Holy Ghost will enable him to be the Christian God wants him to be. These factors are significant to sustain, purify, and control our relationships with the Heavenly Father. The starting point of everyone's experience and relationship with God is faith. It is the foundation of everything that we receive from God. "For I say, through the grace given unto me, to every man that is among you, not to think of himself more highly than he ought to think; but to think soberly, according to as God hath dealt with every man the measure of faith" (Romans 12:3). Since God dealt us the measure of faith, what we do with it, and how we develop it is all-important.

Healing is a general term that includes divine, medical, alternative, and natural methods. When a person is sick, he often seeks relief as soon as possible and the most convenient way – he wants to get well as quickly as possible. Sickness and pain often cause a person to try almost anything to get well. No situation or condition is hopeless as long as we can touch Jesus. To press through the crowd is often the difference between receiving healing or remaining sick. The group represents all the things that are between us and victory. Capernaum, a prosperous fishing town on the Sea of Galilee – became the scene for one of the most significant faith tests during the New Testament times. Like Jairus, we often struggle with situations that are both perplexing and discouraging. Our road in life seems scattered with unexpected pitfalls and unanticipated problems. Whatever the need, God rewards steadfast faith. Like Jairus, we must boldly express the urgent request of our hearts. We must come to the Lord with great determination and confidence in what He can do.

As Christians, our most significant underlying motive should be to please our Savior. We want our lives to reflect the values of Christ. Our day-to-day existence should reflect the things the Lord values and goals He deems worthy of our efforts. So, occasionally the wise Christian should carefully examine his priorities. He should consider them in the light of the Holy Scriptures. He is cautious that his culture does not subtly influence him and cause him to lose proper focus. The most excellent teacher of all times placed much emphasis on prayer. Jesus not only taught individuals how to pray, but He also practiced it. There is scriptural evidence that He prayed early in the morning, late at night, and sometimes all night. Jesus prayed before He ate, before making a decision, and before He performed miracles. He prayed privately and publicly. According to the admonition of the Word of God, Jesus lived according to the Word of God, "In all thy ways acknowledge him, and he shall direct thy path" (Proverbs 3:6). His immortal words, "Men ought always to pray, and not faint" (Luke 18:1), were not merely words; they were His way of life – a life He wants us to imitate.

The Bible is like no other book known to man. It is unique that it is the only Book of its kind written over 1600 years by forty authors who came from all different walks of life – yet the Bible never contradicts itself. Many thousands of writings have come and gone; this Book of books has never faded away. Like no other manual, the Bible affects all people and societies. Where it is honored - life is elevated to a higher standard. Where it is rejected – there is often regression and increased poverty. As Christians, we must not underestimate the enormous value of God's Word – it should lead us in every area of our lives. "Thy word is a lamp unto my feet, and a light unto my path" (Psalm 119:105).

CHAPTER 1

Putting God First

Putting God's Kingdom First

Jesus taught that God's kingdom is an inner spiritual kingdom that is invisible to the natural eye and the inherent intellect. He admonished His followers to seek this kingdom first before they seek anything else: "But seek ye first the kingdom of God, and his righteousness, and all these things shall be added unto you" (Matthew 6:33). As the disciples followed Jesus, they became aware that He had an invisible, inner strength and power. When they sensed that He drew upon this power through prayer – they requested that He teach them to pray. Jesus responded by giving the disciples an example in which we are to pray for God's kingdom to come: "And he said unto them, When ye pray, say, Our Father which art in heaven, hallowed be thy name. Thy kingdom comes. Thy will be done, as in heaven, so on earth" (Luke 11:2). Jesus made it clear that God's kingdom is the fundamental source of spiritual life and strength, and His followers are to partake of this eternal source.

When Jesus taught the disciples to pray – He explained that we must pray for God's rule in our lives. A kingdom entails a system of government and authority. It has a ruler -the king and subjects who must submit to the king. This kingdom also has laws of order that form its structure (Erickson 2015, 274-275)[1]. These laws of order are divine principles of living. The Scriptures refer to these principles as the law, the testimony, the statutes, the commandments, and the Judgment of God: "The law of the LORD is perfect, converting the soul: the testimony of the LORD is sure, making wise the simple. The statutes of the LORD are right, rejoicing the heart: the commandment of the LORD is pure, enlightening the eyes" (Psalm

---

[1] Millard J. Erickson. *Introducing Christian Doctrine*. Grand Rapids, Michigan. Baker Academic. 2015. Pg. 274-275.

19:7-8). To seek first the kingdom of God – we must acknowledge God as king and ruler of our lives. Additionally, we must be willing to learn obedience by submitting our carnal nature to His divine will.

The Scriptures plainly states: "For my thought are not your thought, neither are your ways my ways, saith the LORD. For as the heavens are higher than the earth, so are my ways higher than your ways, and my thoughts than your thoughts" (Isaiah 55:8-9). The divine principles of the kingdom of God vastly differ from the natural laws of this life. Many people have come to view the pursuit of things in this life from the vantage point of self-esteem and self-glory. But such self-promotion too often leads to greed. Even natural laws are continually bent and broken in human society to gain material possessions and acclaim. It seems that human beings generally endeavor to present a particular image of self that they believe will bring the best posture, the most material benefits, the highest status, and all the pleasures this world can give. However, Jesus taught us to seek the kingdom of God first. He wants to reveal the real values of life and deliver humanity from worldly pursuits' delusion. Jesus taught that a person would fall if he fails to build his house upon the rock – referring to His teaching, which embodies the principles of God's kingdom in (Matthew 7:24-27). The difference in this world's human laws and those of God's kingdom is illustrated by the words and life of Jesus as dealt with by the disciples on this particular subject.

The Lord not only taught about putting the principles of the kingdom of God first in our lives – He exemplified it in His own life. The most excellent illustration of all is His death, burial, and resurrection. Jesus lived daily to serve and to help others. He brought healing, salvation, deliverance and contribute to the suffering throughout His ministry. In the wilderness, Jesus denied the satanic lures to high, earthly position and power. In rejecting Satin's tempting offers, He submitted Himself to God's plan that ended on the whipping post and the cross, "And being found in fashion as a man, he humbled himself and became obedient unto death, even the death of the cross" (Philippians 2:8). Jesus could have called legions of angels to rescue him – yet He submitted to His mission that called for His death. Therefore, God highly exalted Him and gave Him a name above every name. The Scriptures points this out: "For whosoever exalteth himself shall be abased; and he that humbleth himself shall be exalted" (Luke 14:11).

Putting God's First Commandment First

An individual interested in pleasing God in our day might ask – which is the greatest commandment. The answer is still the same today as recorded in the first century: "And one of the scribes came, and having heard them reasoning together, and perceiving that he had answered them well, asked him, which is the first commandment of all? And Jesus answered him, the first of all the commandments is, Hear, O Israel; the Lord our God is one Lord: and thou shalt love the Lord thy God with all thy heart, and with all thy soul, and with all thy mind, and with all thy strength: this the first commandment" (Mark 12:28-30). The most important thing we can do for God is to love Him with all our heart, soul, mind, and strength (Conner 1980, 151-152)[2]. People often tend to respond to God's command for us to love Him with all our being with an adverse reaction. We must realize that we are not to live after the carnal nature; conversely, through Christ, we can do all things. Moreover, if we reject the commandment as unattainable – we leave that which is most important - God! If we are determined to overcome our fears of failures and to trust God that He would not require anything of us that is unattainable – we will comprehend what God will do for us.

One of Satin's most effective deceptions is to make a Christian feel that he cannot live for God. God commands that we love Him, but Satan whispers a lie of guilt that causes many to question their relationship to God because of their fluctuating emotional feelings. Since man is an emotional creature – his opinions are not static; instead, they sometimes shift dramatically. In times of emotional stress, Satan tries to convince individuals that they cannot obey God and do not love Him with all their hearts. God's commandment for us to love Him is not based solely on feelings but on our obedience to His commandments. Jesus said: "He

---

[2] Kevin J. Conner., M.Div., Th.D. *The Foundations of Christian Doctrine: A Practical Guide to Christian Belief.* Portland, Oregon. City Christian Publishing. 1980 Pg. 151-152

that hath my commandments, and keepeth them, he it is that love me: and he that loveth me shall be loved of my Father, and I will love him, and will manifest myself to him" (John 14:21). God's command for us to love Him is a command to do something – not merely to feel something. The kind of love that Jesus teaches us to have is agape love, which means to give sacrificially. When we obey God by sacrificing our own will, we are loving God. Jesus is the perfect and complete example of agape love. He prayed in the garden until His will was subdued to that of the Father. To love God with all the heart, mind, soul, and strength includes submitting to the kingdom laws, obeying God's eternal Word, and recognizing His all-knowing will.

Loving God is not an option but is essential if we are to reside in His kingdom. This first and greatest commandment is the crucial Christian priority to God in a personal sense (Scott 2008, 110)[3]. God is a jealous God – He demands that His people be faithful to Him - for when they turn to fake gods, they are like an unfaithful wife. He considers the failure of His people to put Him first to be unfaithfulness. Jesus demonstrated His demand for faithfulness in dealing with the apostle Peter. He gave Peter special attention and prayer in order to establish him as an apostle. Just before Peter's denial and betrayal, Jesus told Peter that Satan desired to have him, but He had prayed for him that his faith would not fail (Luke 22:31-32). Peter responded that he would go to prison or even to death for the Lord. Jesus then forewarned Peter that he would deny Him three times before the chicken would crow. In fulfilling the words of Jesus – Peter denied any knowledge of Him and demonstrated a short-coming in his love for the Lord. After the resurrection, Peter announced to the other disciples that he was going fishing (John 21:3). After the disciples had spent a night fishing in vain – Jesus appeared to them and enabled them to make a great catch of fish. After cooking their breakfast of fish on the fire – Jesus asked Peter if he loved Him more than the fish – perhaps referring to the fishing business. Peter's response was in the affirmative, but Jesus pursued the questioning further. A second and then a third time, Jesus questioned Peter's love for Him. Finally, Peter was grieved, probably

---

[3] Steven K. Scott. *The Greatest Words Ever Spoken: Everything Jesus Said about You, Your Life, and Everything Else.* Colorado Springs, Colorado. Water Brook Press. 2008. Pg. 110.

remembering his earlier failures. Jesus wanted to use Peter as an apostle, but He demanded from Peter the kind of love that would put God first and produce unswerving loyalty and faithfulness.

Not only is loving God required of us and vital to Him in a personal way, but loving God is the proper response to His love for us. Because He first loved us – we are capable of loving Him. He loved us while we were unlovable. When we return His love, a special bond is created between God and us – allowing us to benefit richly—putting God first promises to bring reward to the person who loves Him. The apostle John referred to himself in his gospel as the disciple whole Jesus loved (John 21:7). Jesus loved all the disciples, and He loves every sinner, and He died on the cross to make it possible for everyone to be saved. But perhaps there was something special about John's relationship with Jesus. For example, he sat next to the Lord at the table and asked the Master the question of who would betray Him. Again, when Jesus was on the cross, it was John whom he appointed to care for His mother (John 19:25-27). The love between the Lord and John is typical of our relationship with Him when we love Him supremely. Having a loving relationship with Jesus is difficult for sinners to conceive. Yet God in His Great mercy has placed Himself within the grasp of every person who will put Him first and who will love Him with all his heart, mind, soul, and strength.

Putting God First Through Faith

Putting God's kingdom first and putting God's first commandment first involve acting by faith. To submit to His kingdom laws, humbling oneself before Him – demand an of faith in God's goodness give us His best. To love the Lord with all the heart, mind, soul, and strength, while our feeling may sometimes struggle to comply, is also an act of faith. Yet exercising faith is serving God. The writer of Hebrews stated, "Without faith, it is impossible to please him," and again, "the just shall live by faith" (Hebrews 10:38). Indeed, when an individual puts God first in his or her life – it is faith. Loving God and living in submission to Him are both acts of faith; believing in God puts Him first in our lives. As believers, we are admonished to honor the name of Son God – to believe in the name of Jesus Christ. "And this is His commandment, that we should believe on his son Jesus Christ" (I John 3:23). This is not a new commandment to believe in the name of Jesus Christ; instead, it is in part a fulfillment of the command to love God with all of our beings. Since obeying God and submitting ourselves to Him require the believer to act in faith, it follows that believing in the name of Jesus Christ, in a practical sense, includes loving Him with all the heart, mind, soul, and strength.

CHAPTER 2

Praying Effectually

Command to Pray

Some may ask the question, why did Jesus pray if He was God in the flesh? There are several reasons why he prayed. The human element is that the man Christ Jesus needed fellowship with the Father. Another reason was that he prayed because he is our supreme example, and we are to follow in His footsteps. "And in the morning, rising up a great while before day, he went out and departed into a solitary place, and there prayed" (Mark 1:35). The Scriptures are full of examples of Christ's prayers. The Bible gives examples of all-night prayer sessions (Luke 6:12). Jesus prayed at the tomb of Lazarus. He prayed and blessed a small boy's lunch before feeding the multitude. On numerous occasions, Jesus prayed for the sick and afflicted. He prayed for the disciples in the upper room before departing for Gethsemane. He prayed in Gethsemane and also for His enemies while hanging on the cross. In His humanity, prayer was Christ's source of power and strength (Cardwell 2014, 15-16). Even though He was God manifested in the flesh, Jesus received power and direction through prayer. He continually ministered to the needs of others. In His humanity, [4]Jesus recognized His dependence on the Father. Prayer was His lifeline, and it is also our today. Effectual praying is necessary to be successful in this most crucial time in our lives. Jesus prayed – we must pray also.

Praying is the appropriate way to communicate with our Heavenly Father. It is a heavenly conduit that is used to petition God when we have spiritual or earthly needs. We can ask in faith then believe that God will meet our needs according to His will. "And this is the confidence that we have in him, that, if we ask anything according to his will, he heareth us:

---

[4] Jon J. Cardwell. *Lord Teach Us to Pray: A Devotional Study of Christ's Model Prayer for His Disciples.* Jessup, Maryland. Vayahiy Press. 2014. Pg. 15-16.

And if we know that he hears us, whatsoever we ask, we know that we have the petitions that we desired of him" (I John 5:14-15) (Smith 2016, 65)[5]. Jesus commanded His followers to pray. In His famous discourse, the Sermon on Mount, He said, "When you pray," not "If you pray." Prayer is not an option for Christians – Christ made it clear that He expects us to pray. Jesus Challenged us to pray when He said, "Ask, and it shall be given you; seek, and ye shall find; knock, and it shall be opened unto you" (Luke 11:9). If we do not ask, He probably will not give to us. When the disciples were unable to cast out the demons from the child that was brought to them – Jesus told them that this kind of spiritual conquest is accomplished only by fasting and prayer (Matthew 17:16-21). To meet the challenges in this generation, the church must fast and pray. There is a resurgence in malicious activity and worship. Morality and decency are in decay and disarray. We must actively pray more so that we will have the power of God to face these situations.

The commands of Jesus to pray were emphatic enough that they had a profound effect upon His followers – who saw the impact of prayer in the ministry of Jesus and realized the power of prayer. As Jesus was preparing to ascend to heaven at the close of His earthly ministry – He instructed His disciples to return to Jerusalem and wait there for the Holy Ghost. Perhaps five hundred people were in attendance that day – yet only one hundred twenty were in the upper room in Acts chapter 2. Those who willingly obeyed the command of Jesus to pray were the ones who received the promised Holy Ghost on the Day of Pentecost. There are no set times to pray unless you have selected times accordingly within a prayer strategy plan. However, we must always allow the Holy Spirit to guide us and lead us into prayer. It is the Holy Spirit who ushers us into the presence of God. Our lifestyle should be one of continually praying; therefore, the custom of kneeling is not a requirement for presenting ourselves to God. Communicating in prayer is just one facet of our relationship with God. We can approach Him as the need arise and as prompted by the Holy Spirit. Even though Jesus is not in our midst physically today – He speaks through the avenue of His Word, His Spirit, and the mouth of the

---

[5] Gwendolyn Smith. *Praying Effectively at Source: A 7-Key Prayer Model.* Middletown, DE. Sheba Publication. 2016. Pg. 65.

ministry. Prayer prepares us for each of these avenues of communication from God, and prayer facilitates the process.

To pray continually does not mean that we must pray for all our waking hours verbally nonstop – for that would be virtually impossible. Our working hours and family duties prevent us from verbally praying all the time. We must pay attention to our required responsibilities in these areas, which is spiritually right for us to do. There are seasons of prayer when we pray for extended lengths of time. On most days, however, Christians usually follow their established prayer pattern – having a specific time set aside to pray and focus on God. Christians should live in an attitude of prayerfulness. Even while doing other tasks –prayer can be in our hearts. Praise and worship can be welling up within us, and we can live in an attitude of God-awareness. For some, their jobs would allow them to sing praises to God while working and still not hinder their job performance. All of us can be prayerful as we work. Just a "Thank you, Jesus," and a "Hallelujah" as we work helps keep our mind focused upon the Lord. We have a promise of peace if our mind has stayed upon Him: "Thou wilt keep him in perfect peace, whose mind is stayed on thee: because he trusteth in thee" (Isaiah 26:3).

According to Gwendolyn Smith in her book *"Praying Effectively at Source: A 7Key Prayer Model,"* "Prayer is not only vocalized, but one can meditate or pray without the expression of words." Hannah was the wife of Elkanah – a serving priest. She was barren and yearned for her womb to be opened by the Lord. In her deep affliction, she prayed to the Lord – weeping bitterly in the presence of the high priest Eli as he sat by post in the Temple of the Lord (I Samuel 1:10). Eli was well in age, and his spiritual effectiveness was undesirable before God. He misunderstood Hannah for being drunken. "Now Hannah, she spake in her heart; only her lips moved, but her voice was not heard: therefore, Eli thought she had been drunken" (1 Samuel 1:13). Out of a distressed spirit, she stated, "No, my lord – I am not drunk, but a woman troubled in spirit." But when Eli saw that she was in fervent prayer – he blessed her. God granted Hannah's request, and her son Samuel was born the following year. Having a prayerful attitude must not be the total sum of our praying – we need a particular time without interruption to focus our attention on the Lord in Prayer. We must have time for personal devotions to communicate daily with the

Lord. Continual prayer also refers to consistent prayer over a period that becomes a part of our life's routine. It has been said that if a person does something long regularly enough – it becomes a habit. Habits can be good or harmful. However, prayer is a good habit as long as it does not become commonplace, stale, or lose its vitality. Each time we kneel in prayer, even though we may have been doing it for years – we must approach God with admiration, reverence, and respect.

Continual prayer is an essential element in victorious living. People who pray usually have little trouble in living a victorious life. They have learned to walk in the Spirit and overcome the fleshly appetites seeking to allure them with temptation. Through prayer, they have strength enough to ward off the enemy of their souls. "Men ought always to pray and not to faint" (Luke 18:1). Fainting is a sign of weakness and lack of strength. If people pray continually instead of sporadically – they will not be troubled with spiritual fainting. Jesus said we ought always to pray. Prayer is not an exercise that we reserve for slack, unoccupied periods in our lives. Praying is not optional for the child of God. Other things may have to be left undone so that we can pray and maintain our spiritual strength. God wants us to pray, and He wants to answer our prayers, but He makes our use of prayer as a privilege to communicate with His help of worship as a discipline. To receive answers to prayer – we must meet God's terms. If we neglect His commandments - our petitions will not be honored. He will alter situations only at the request of obedient and humble souls (Tozer 2008, 92-94)[6].

Encouragement to Pray

Apostle James, in his epistle, placed great emphasis on prayer. He gave a pattern to follow when we are afflicted or sick. If a person is afflicted, he is to pray. If a person is sick – he is to call for the elders of the church to pray over him, anointing him with oil in the name of the Lord. (James 5:13-14). Many illnesses that ended in death during James's time could be treated by modern medical technology – yet any sickness, whether or

---

[6] A. W. Tozer. *Man: The Dwelling Place of God*. Chicago, Illinois. Wing Spread Publisher. 2008. Pg. 92-94.

not it is life-threatening, still causes concern and alarm. It is imperative now, as it was then, that we pray an effectual prayer for each other's needs. James made a difference between those afflicted and those who are sick. To the afflicted, James said to pray. But to those who are sick, he said for them to call for the elders of the church and ask them to pray and anoint them with oil in the name of the Lord Jesus. To call for the elders is an act of faith. Faith is a requirement to receive anything from God. It is not the ministry's place to reach the sick and volunteer to come and pray for them (Bosworth 1993, 55)[7]. The written pattern to follow is for the sick to exercise their faith by calling for prayer. This does not mean that God will not heal unless a person calls for the elders – God may heal even when another saint prays or even when he is not anointed. But this promise gives the sick biblical authority to call for church leaders and a way to exercise his faith in God.

We can be confident and assured that if we obey the Scriptures – we will receive the answer to our prayers, whether for healing or other needs. Jesus never fails. when we earnestly seek – we shall find, and when we persistently knock – the doors will be opened to us. (Luke 11:9-10). For our prayers to avail much, we must meet certain conditions and criteria. The Scriptures are not vague and unclear regarding this subject. Principles of answered prayer are established in the Scriptures. First of all, we must pray with a clean heart. I order for prayers to be effective – we must be able to approach God with a clear conscience and with no unconfessed sins in our hearts. "He that covereth his sins shall not prosper" (Proverbs 28:13). "If I regard iniquity in my heart, the Lord will not hear me" (Psalm 66:18). Without guilt or condemnation present, we can come with boldness and confidence to God in prayer. If there is hatred or unkind feeling towards someone – we must remove those feelings before praying is effectual. John wrote much about our relationship with God and our brethren. We must be right with God and right with each other also.

Secondly, we must pray with faith. Children often receive things from God quickly and easily since their faith has not been diluted with human reasoning. They believe God when they pray in such a simple, honest, and straightforward manner. To be effective in prayer, we must have the same

---

[7] F. F. Bosworth. *Christ The Healer*. Grand Rapids, Michigan. Fleming H. Revell. Baker Book House Co. 1993. Pg. 55.

simplicity of faith that a child possesses. We should not try to reason faith out of the situation. James said, "But let him ask in faith, nothing wavering. For he that wavereth is like a wave of the sea driven with the wind and tossed" (James 1:6). Israel failed to receive many promises of God due to their continual unbelief. God was insulted by their lack of faith. He had never failed them – they had no reason to doubt His power of faithfulness. Their many experiences should have taught them to have faith in God. If doubts consume us – we should ask God to increase our faith. God can use our little faith – even faith as small as a mustard seed to work miracles in our lives. We must pray with faith for prayer to be effectual.

Thirdly, we must pray in Jesus' name (Wagner 1996, 125-130)[8]. In James 5:14, the elders are instructed to anoint the sick in the name of the Lord Jesus. By invoking the excellent name of Jesus – we expect the mighty power of God to be brought into our situation. Through the ages, mighty men of God faced formidable foes and conquered them in the name of the Lord. As he faced the taunting abuses of Goliath, the young warrior proclaimed that he was coming in the name of the Lord. The Lord worked a great victory for David and Israel on that day. Peter and John performed a healing miracle for the lame man at the gate of the Temple, which is called Beautiful, by calling on the name of Jesus. The man's ankle bones received instant strength, and the man followed the two apostles into the Temple, walking, leaping, and praising God. When a multitude gathered, Peter told them, "And His name through faith in his name hath made this man strong, whom ye see and know" (Acts 3:16).

Next, we must pray with fervency—the word fervent means to be intense, passionate, devoted, and enthusiastic. Earnest prayer is praying with feeling and sincerity. God does not answer a prayer that is offered halfhearted, but He will not turn away the humble and contrite seeker. Fervency may be manifested with physical expressions such as tears, changes in voice inflection, and even physical trembling – but it is always a condition of the heart rather than the body's movement that influences God. Lastly, we must pray with persistence. In Luke 18, Jesus gave us the parable of the widow and the unjust judge. When He always said to pray and not to faint – He described the widow's persistence in her

---

[8] Peter C. Wagner. *Spiritual Warfare Strategy: Confronting Spiritual Powers.* Shippensburg, PA. Destiny Image Publishing, Inc. 1996. Pg. 125-130.

efforts to gain satisfaction from the judge. She refused to quit, and her relentlessly pleading her cause finally moved the unjust judge to grant her petition. Similarly, in Matthew 15:21-28, a Canaanite woman persisted in her request when the Lord rebuffed her. With beautiful humility, faith, and persistence – she refused to accept no for an answer. Her praying was effectual and fervent. Unless we feel that God has given us a final solution – we should feel free to return again and again to Him with our requests. After Elijah prayed six times, there was no sign of rain. But the seventh time he prayed – his servant saw the cloud that assured Elijah the victory. What if he had given up before the seventh time? We, too, must be persistent in our prayer requests.

Jacob was a man of passionate longing for spiritual matters. We may fault him for his deceptive nature but not for his desire for God. He wanted the birthright, and he wanted the blessing of the firstborn, which he received by deception. Later in his life, he wrestled through the night with the angel of God as he sought a blessing. Because he refused to let the angel go until he was blessed – his life was forever changed. Though anointed to be king of Israel as a teenager – David had many years of maturing before he ascended to the throne. During the waiting years, he learned to rely upon the Lord, and prayer and praise were the sources of strength for him. David wrote many beautiful and heart probing psalms as his emotions ran from utter despair to soaring faith. As the weight of life's emotions pulled at his heart – his prayers helped stabilize his faith and walk with God. Elijah was called a man of "like passion" as we are, yet he prayed and received results. He prayed fervently and effectually, and he was a righteous man. Though the prayer on Mount Carmel was of short duration – it brought the fire from heaven.

Rewards of Prayer

Jesus told us that if we ask, we will receive it. We can ask and receive what we need, or we can doubt and do without. The rewards of prayer include having our needs supplied. It is also rewarding to pray for others and see God answer our prayers on their behalf – meeting their needs. We know that we must rely upon God, for without Him, we are helpless. But it is fulfilling and rewarding to see that we can have a part in helping others by our praying for them. We know that we are saved by grace and not by works, but on that day, when we stand in the kingdom of God, we will perhaps understand more how our lives and our prayers have blessed others. The Scripture says that God will reward us for our labors of love. We will hear Him say, "Well done, good and faithful servant." One tangible reward of praying is having specific needs met. These needs may range from a minor problem to life-threatening situations; however, God is concerned about all of our life's issues – not merely significant crises. The restoration of physical health when one is healed is a reward of prayer. By our prayers, God unites us together to minister to each other when sickness comes. The person receiving prayer is healed and gains an appreciation for other members of the church.

The rewards of receiving prayer from one person may include renewed strength as a Christian prays for him with intercession. Unsaved loved ones often find God when a faithful relative of a friend seeks God for their salvation. Others are protected by God when they are in danger because someone touched God in prayer on their behalf (Kendrick 2015, 194-197)[9]. Christians never outgrow their need for prayer. Though some are blessed with a special ministry of prayer – all saints of God need to know how to pray effectually. Jesus gave us a perfect example by which to pattern our lives. He emphasized prayer both by example and by teaching. Jesus Christ commanded us to pray always. He spoke of the necessity of persistent and consistent prayer. He rebuked His disciples when they loved slumber more than prayer in Gethsemane – for He encouraged them to pray during this stressful hour of His trial. They learned their lesson well – for, after the Day of Pentecost, they became people of prayer. God's Word sets the guidelines so we do not have to stumble through life being deficient in vital areas of Christian living. We only need to bow our hearts before God in faith, earnestly seek His blessing, make our request known to Him, and receive all provisions to meet our needs.

---

[9] Stephen and Alex Kendrick. *The Battle Plan for Prayer: From Basic Training to Targeted Strategies.* Nashville, Tennessee. B & H Publishing Group. 2015. Pg. 194-197.

CHAPTER 3

Practicing Forgiveness

Forgiveness Commanded

Forgiveness is crucial to Christianity. Jesus taught us that if we do not forgive others, we will not be forgiven by God. As Jesus forgave us, so are we to forgive others. Jesus prayed, "And forgive us our debts, as we forgive of debtors" (Matthew 6:12). Not only does this teach that God wants us to forgive others, but it also implies that: a) each time we pray – we stand as examples of God's love by forgiving all others; b) we should make forgiveness a daily practice; and c) we are forgiven as we forgive others; in other words, only as we forgive others will our heavenly Father forgive us. Not only does the Lord's Prayer imply that we can receive forgiveness only if we forgive others, but it is also plainly taught in other verses. "For if ye forgive men their trespasses, your heavenly Father will also forgive you: but if ye forgive not men their trespasses, neither will your Father forgive your trespasses" (Matthew 6:14-15).

Most Christians have no difficulty in forgiving once or twice. Still, when the same offense occurs several times, some Christians begin to convince themselves that it is permissible to stop forgiving. Christ taught us that we should forgive as often as our brother sins against us. This was a response to Peter's question, "Then came Peter to him, and said, Lord, how oft shall my brother sin against me, and I forgive him? Till seven times? Jesus saith unto him, I say not unto thee, Until seven times: but, until seventy times seven" (Matthew 18:21-22). Moreover, anyone who would take a scorecard and keep count up to four hundred and ninety times is ridiculous. It is equally ludicrous to think that Jesus meant for us to keep score up to that number. On the contrary, He used a figure of speech to show that we should continue to forgive – even if violated hundreds of times literally.

Forgiveness Offered

To forgive men of crimes for which restitution can be made is a good thing, but to forgive men of deeds for which no amount of correction can right the wrong is more than okay – it is incredible. The song uses the best adjective when it calls God's grace "Amazing Grace." But in offering forgiveness to Judas for his act of betrayal, Christ did more than impress us with His grace; He left us an example that we should follow. Maybe most men can claim to have been betrayed in one way or another, but in every act of betrayal, no matter how horrible the results of the action, Christ left us an example of what to do – forgive the betrayer (Wagner, Warfare Prayer 1992, 121-122)[10]. Unfortunately, like many sinners today, Judas did not respond to Jesus' offer of forgiveness. Although in his condemnation, Judas sought to undo his betrayal – he did repent within himself for the betrayal of the Lord Jesus, "Then Judas, which had betrayed him, when he saw that he was condemned, repented himself, and brought the thirty pieces of silver again to the chief priests and elders, saying, I have sinned in that I have betrayed innocent blood. And they said, what is that to us? See thou to that" (Matthew 27:3-4). Thus, Christ's offer of life was rejected, and sin worked its destruction in him. Judas could have been saved, but he disregarded the one hope of salvation.

It was marvelous that Jesus Christ was willing to forgive the one who was responsible for His capture. But it may stagger us to see Him in excruciating agony, hanging on a cross of shame, and praying kindly for those who are responsible for His pain, "Then said Jesus, Father, forgive them; for they know not what do. And they parted his raiment and cast lots" (Luke 23:34). However, this example of Christ's spirit of forgiveness challenges us to follow His leadership. What Christ did must be emulated by those who claim to follow Him. If a Christian is crucified today – whether on a cross, by the news media, by rumor and scandal, or by any other means – his response should be no less than that of Jesus. He should pray for the forgiveness of those who despitefully use him. Pastors counsel thousands of people across the country, and most will agree that the ability to forgive would solve many crises. Marriages have dissolved by record

---

[10] Peter C. Wagner. *Warfare Prayer: How to Seek God's Power and Protection in the Battle to Build His Kingdom.* Ventura, California. Regal Books. 1992. Pg. 121-122.

numbers, not so much because of adultery, lying, or careless behavior, but as for the unwillingness of one partner to forgive the other for his or her sins. Likewise, parents and children sometimes separate for no more significant reason than the stubborn refusal of one to back down and ask forgiveness or to extend mercy to the other.

Forgiveness in Action

It is incredible how many people involved in a conflict with another person will say something like this, "I forgive them, but I cannot forget what they have done." It is impossible for us to completely forget to eliminate an injustice committed to us from our human minds. However, it is possible to completely forgive that the only time the memory is ever activated is when we are benefiting someone else by our own experiences or when something positive can come from the misdeeds' minds. To forgive, therefore, is not necessarily to forget. However, to forgive others is not something done with words only but with positive actions. When we genuinely forgive, we demonstrate forgiveness in several powerful ways. Jesus taught us to "Love your enemies, bless them that curse you, do good to them that hate you, and pray for them which despitefully use you, and persecute you" (Matthew 5:44). It is commonly observed that one can love with their lips only, saying they love someone who has offended them. Some make it a point to tell as many as possible that they have no ill-will toward anyone. Jesus taught us to do more than merely say that we forgive or say that we love (Placher 2013, 52, 257)[11]. He taught us to pray for those who use or abuse us. Praying for such people does lovely things.

The first good act we can perform toward those who wrong us is to pray for them. Beyond that, we can find ways to express a desire to continue our friendship. Regardless of our relationship with the other person – we can find ways to be agreeable. Sometimes the injured person is a husband or wife. In such cases, it is easier to perform acts of kindness because we have ongoing relationships with our spouses, and we are in daily contact. Sometimes the rift comes between people who work together, and again

---

[11] William Placher and Derek R. Nelson. *A History of Christian Theology: An Introduction*. Louisville, Kentucky. Westminster John Knox Press. 2013. Pg. 52, 257.

the regular contact makes it easier to show acts of kindness toward the injured person. For example, one man felt that his supervisor had misled him – that he had been betrayed in not getting a recommendation for promotion at a particular time. His first reaction was to try to go over his boss's head and complain to a superior. After thinking it over, he decided that such an action might result in worsening his work environment. Finally, he resorted to the Word of God and decided to try to obey it honestly. Using Jesus' command to "bless them that curse you," he set out to be a blessing to his supervisor. He worked harder than he had worked before. He never brought up his feelings, other than the one time he brought it up to apologize for jumping to conclusions about the boss' motives. When he heard someone else criticizing the boss, he tried to defend him. If he felt he could not take the boss's point of view – he merely stayed out of the conversation. In time, the boss recommended him for a promotion – which he soon received. By the time the upgrade came, the Christian honestly admitted to his boss that it was good he had not been promoted earlier. He had needed a certain maturity that could not have been developed within the crucible of leadership but had to be possessed before entering the leadership's arena.

It is possible to pray for others and even do real acts of kindness toward them and keep an unpleasant feeling toward them in one's heart. Forgiveness must be accompanied by a tender, merciful heart toward those we forgive. "Be ye kind one to another, tenderhearted, forgiving one another, even as God for Christ's sake hath forgiven you" (Ephesians 4:32). The word forgiveness comes from the Greek word eusplagchnos, which, according to Strong's Exhaustive Concordance, means "well-compassioned and sympathetic." With Christ's help, we may also find that we feel genuine concern and compassion for the very people who offend us. Tenderheartedness is not shown merely by a humble tone of voice or a specific cast-down look. Religious "actors" can affect such behavior. A tender heart is reflected in kind replies when speaking to the offender and refusing to criticize or gossip about the person to another.

When we consider the debt, we owe to God and that debt has been paid by Him – we must humble and sufficiently repay that act by forgiving others. Whoever has been offended – is his or her offense higher than that which he committed against God? Yet God has forgiven us all. We must not see ourselves as better than we are. It was not a good thing when a Christian is saved from horrible sins to become arrogant once the blood cleanses them of Jesus Christ. However, Christ's cleansing blood was not meant to make us proud. On the contrary, it should bring gratefulness and humility. Likewise, our act of forgiving others seldom produces arrogance in them; it usually causes them to respond with gentleness and meekness.

The Fruit of Forgiveness

Beautiful things result when we follow the Bible's mandate to forgive others. The first intent in forgiveness is to restore the broken friendship. Reconciliation is evidence of mercy. Sometimes the church develops an idea that the world needs to see more miracles from the Christians. If they could see more miracles of healings – we as the Christian community think that we would be able to win our friends and relatives to the cause of Christ. Notwithstanding, more people are won to God by or love toward each other more than by miracles that happen among us. Yes, the church believes in the miraculous power of God to heal and deliver, yet we must also believe in and practice forgiveness. When Christian couples divorce over matters similar to those outside the church, it reveals a severe failure of the values. The church must rise above the standards of the world – especially in this area of forgiveness. It is far more convincing to non-believers that a person's Christianity works when he is seen being reconciled to someone who had offended him than when he is heard testifying that he believes in the mighty power of God. Restored relationships give apparent credibility to our genuine faith and God's absolute power more than notable miracles do.

Forgiveness bolsters our effectiveness in witnessing. A leading pastor in North Carolina challenged his congregation to win one enemy during a year. The apparent lesson he wanted them to learn was that a person could not win enemies to Christ – we must first make the enemy a friend. Enemies can be won by Jesus Christ only after they become friends. Forgiveness is the miraculous agent that transforms enemies into friends. Then Christ is lifted for all to see. In reality, no one would welcome another's invitation to his church or tolerate the pressure about his faith if he knew the one witness was also harboring bitterness toward him or another person. However, anyone appreciated the fact that others may have had their bitter quarrels – providing they have overcome them and now allow love to live where hatred once did. In an environment of forgiveness, Jesus always comes out as the winner - He is lifted up. The average man in the world knows how difficult it is to forgive when he is hurt. When he sees a Christian freely forgive others – he knows that person is a genuine Christian.

Much could be said about the effect of forgiveness has on an individual's witness and the general well-being of those receiving the witness. The one who offers forgiveness also reaps a personal benefit from the act. He or she gets a sense of peace that cannot be found as long as any root of bitterness dwells within him or her. The Bible teaches that any "root of bitterness" will both trouble us and defile others: "Looking diligently lest any man fails of the grace of God; lest any root of bitterness springing up trouble you, and thereby many be defiled" (Hebrews 12:15). The caution is preceded by a plea to "follow peace with all men." To refuse the path of peace in resolving differences and effecting a reconciliation with those estranged due to problems is suffering from the loss of inner peace and inviting bitterness with all of its destructive performances.

Asking Forgiveness of Others

Up to this point, we have primarily dealt with forgiving those who have offended us. It is equally essential to recognize the value of asking forgiveness when we have done wrong (Wagner, Praying with Power 1997, 116-119)[12]. Most pastors have to deal with at least two people who were angry with each other. They usually discover that each person privately will admit that they should ask or offer forgiveness from each other. However, when the two confront each other, their stubbornness and pride prevent both persons from taking the first step toward forgiveness. According to Peter C. Wagner, in his book *"Praying with Power: How to Pray Effectively and Hear Clearly from God,"* "It is possible to go back and confront the wounds that have caused us to hurt from months and even years in past." A

---

[12] Peter C. Wagner. *Praying with Power: How to Pray Effective and Hear Clearly from God. Shippensburg*, PA. Destiny Image Publishing, Inc. 1997. Pg. 116-119

Christian should not expect to go through life without offending anyone – for he eventually will. Therefore, he should have his mind made up that when he does hurt someone, he will be quick to ask forgiveness so that the other person does struggle long with anger and resentment. The Christian is obligated to initiate forgiveness unselfishly.

When we are hurting from an offense, even if we realize we were at fault – the last thing we want is to restore the friendship of the person we are angry with. However, Christ in us continues to work on our feelings inwardly, and He makes us realize that broken relationships must be mended. For the Scripture says: "And they that shall be of thee shall build the old waste places: thou shalt raise the foundations of many generations; and thou shalt be called, the repairer of the breach, the restorer of the paths to dwell in" (Isaiah 58:12). Moreover, the quicker the response to admit one's fault and ask for forgiveness – the easier it is to restore the friendship. As trivial as the fault might have been, if forgiveness is not sought after – it will soon grow out of hand. However, if forgiveness is found quickly, the cause of Christ may not suffer at all. The world knows we are human, that to "err is human," and they accept error to some extent from a Christian. But to seek forgiveness is far-reaching, and it is associated with God's mighty acts, which makes it all the more impressive when a Christian genuinely practices it.

CHAPTER 4

Sincere Prayer

Pattern for Prayer

The disciples, observing the prayer habits of Jesus, requested a lesson in prayer. Under the law, all spiritual or ritual work was left to the priest. The bringing of sacrifices was all that was required of the laity. However, we can and do approach God for ourselves under grace, which is all the more a need to know how to pray. Everyone will stand or fall based on his relationship with God, and that relationship is established and maintained by prayer. The Lord introduces us with a promise in the Scriptures – the promise pertains to several prayer variations. "And I say unto you, Ask, and it shall be given you; seek, and ye shall find; knock, and it shall be opened unto you. For every one that asketh received; and he that seeketh findeth, and to him that knocketh it shall be opened" (Luke 11:9-10). The Bible proclaims that all forms of sincere prayer will be heard – provided they are offered through Jesus Christ and are for promised blessings. So, the prayers grow from asking, which is the statement, to seek, which is the pleading, and then to knock, which is the critical requesting. Uniquely, to each of these stages of prayer, there is a well-defined promise. He who asks will have; What more did he ask for? But he who seeks will go further; he will find, will enjoy, will grasp, and know that he has achieved. He who knocks will go further still, for he will understand, and to him will the treasurable thing be opened (Spurgeon 1998, 17)[13].

There are many excellent books on prayer. *"Spiritual Warfare Strategy: Confronting Spiritual Powers"* by C. Peter Wagner, *"The Battle Plan for Prayer: From Basic Training to Targeted Strategies"* by Stephen and Alex Kendrick, and *"Spurgeon on Prayer and Spiritual Warfare"* by Charles

---

[13] Charles Spurgeon. *Spurgeon on Prayer and Spiritual Warfare*. New Kensington, PA. Whitaker House. 1998. Pg. 17.

Spurgeon are all inspirational and excellent prayer books. These and many other books are tremendous in provoking one to prayer. It is not enough to read these books and realize the need to pray, for prayer can only be done by applying ourselves with all our hearts. Jesus gave an outline for us to follow, similarly molding our praying. First in importance is the attitude we have in approaching God as our heavenly Father – God should always be approached with reverence. With respect, we petition the Almighty as "Our Father." He is a better heavenly Father than we are earthly parents. Being part of the family of God is no small matter. "Furthermore, we have had fathers of our flesh which corrected us, and we gave them reverence: shall we not much rather be in subjected unto the Father of spirits, and live?" (Hebrews 12:9). Since any correction God administers is for our profit, our attitude should be of eagerness, desire, and wiliness. Our heavenly Father is not a fire-breathing tyrant – waiting for us to err so that He can slap us with a vengeance.

Additionally, we must approach God in faith. No one is poor who has learned to use faith. Faith is the "kingdom currency." No matter how much faith a person has used in reaching where he is in Christ, it does not diminish; it multiplies. "Now faith is the substance of things hoped for, the evidence of things not seen" (Hebrews 11:1). Faith in the Gospel produces results (Toon 1996, 120)[14]. One who has obeyed the Gospel does not have to worry over sins of the past - repentance produces forgiveness, and baptism brings about remission of past sins. Moreover, those sins are entirely covered by the blood of Jesus Christ. God does not even remember those blood washed sins. The next step in the process is the Holy Ghost's infilling, which is the Spirit of God within us – the hope of glory. Completely trusting in our heavenly Father, we can come boldly to the throne of grace. With sincerity and genuine love on our part, we develop a lasting relationship and the right attitude toward God.

In light of what God has done, it is only natural that praise should be an integral part of prayer. "Praise waiteth for thee, O God, in Sion: and unto thee shall the vow be performed" (Psalm 65:1). There are many reasons to praise God. We praise Him for hearing and answering our prayers, for pardoning our sins, for giving us blessings, for delivering us

---

[14] Peter Toon. *Our Triune God: A Biblical Portrayal of the Trinity.* Vancouver, British Columbia. Regent College Publishing. 1996. Pg. 120.

from evil and the enemies, and for supplying our needs. There is much praise for accumulated benefits that we should release to God. Especially in those who have the revelation of the name of Jesus Christ – praise should be ever mounting. The announcement of God's plan for the future is also a blessing. We may someday join together with King David, Moses, prophet Isaiah, apostle Paul, and John in singing praise to the infinite wisdom and love of the Lord, by whose counsel of all things were made and will be dominated by Christ's lordship. Through the prophets, the Lord gives His people a heavenly vision of the glory prepared for them, of the kingdom of God in Christ, of the new world, characterized by righteousness, justice, and holiness (VanGemeren 2000, 471).[15]

To be led by the Spirit of God is to dethrone self and place Jesus on the throne of the heart. The Bible states, "The steps of a good man are ordered by the Lord: and he delighted in his way" (Psalm 37:23). It is of the utmost importance who directs our path. If we live our life by our will – the Lord cannot have His way. "For my thoughts are not your thoughts, neither are your ways my ways, saith the LORD. For as the heavens are higher than the earth, so are my ways higher than your ways, and my thoughts than your thoughts" (Isaiah 55:8-9). Just as God has better thoughts and ways than we do, so His will is right for us. The temptation will not come from following the Lord; it comes instead when a person is "drawn away of his own lust, and enticed" (James 1:14). To submit is to yield our lives to God's purpose. Just as Jesus prayed in Gethsemane, "Not my will but Thine be done," so should we pray in like manner. Yielding is more than lip service, for it involves submitting the mind, emotions, and physical self to the Master's service. It is also submitting to the pastor, who is in authority over us. The prayer to lead us not into temptation but deliver us from evil encompasses this aspect of our lives.

Purpose of Prayer

There are many reasons why people pray. First of all, there are many needs that we want God to meet. Some burdens are weighting many

---

[15] Willem Vangemeren. *The Progress of Redemption: The Story of Salvation from Creation to the New Jerusalem.* Grand Rapids, Michigan. Baker Books. 2000. Pg. 471.

of God's people down. People who are in bondage, whether physical or spiritual – yearning for deliverance. Mainly, the primary purpose of prayer is communicating with God. Additionally, according to Willem VanGemeren in his book "*The Progress of Redemption*," "Prayer is also the expression of faith and persistence, as the godly do not give up, but persevere in waiting for their redemption." There is a distinction between those who are Christ's and those who are not. This confidence that we are part of God's family gives us boldness and encourages us in our prayers. This removes the feeling of strain and reluctance about approaching the Father. A true Christian does not feel uncomfortable talking with the Lord. With the confidence that we are in Christ and that He hears us - we are armed with faith. God has freely expressed Himself to us through His Word and by the anointed preaching of the Gospel. We do not have to scrabble in uncertainty as to what God requires. On the other hand, prayer enables us to lay exposed the bad feelings and desires. When we stop praying - we lose our close relationship with God. Something vital goes from us when we lose the touch of God from our lives. The devil clouds our minds with uncertainties. Prayer then becomes a duty rather than a privilege. Instead of building up ourselves by praying in the Holy Ghost – regression begins. Instead of stability, there is wavering. We must keep the lines of communication open to God and pray without ceasing.

Athletes and health enthusiasts spend hours daily lifting weights and doing exercises to develop muscles. Some are so devoted to training that they injure themselves during a workout. If this is done to acquire physical strength, how much more should we be fervently seeking God for renewal and inward force? At a time when compromise and letting down moral standards is the order of the day in many camps – our heartbeat must be exercised to become stronger, to be more like Christ. Prayer is how we may be like Christ. It is an exercise of the soul in developing our "most holy faith." According to Stephen and Alex Kendrick in their book "*The Battle Plan for Prayer: From Basic Training to Targeted Strategies*," "Prayer is an admission that we are not in control, and yet at the same time completely and confidently under God's control." Strength is required to withstand the pressures brought by the power of darkness against the mind. Notably, Eve was deceived into disobedience, but Adam succumbed because of weakness. It is sad not to know what is right, but it is even distressing to know what is right but not have the strength to do it.

Prayer gives us the power to be like Christ and to do that which is right in the sight of God.

A tremendous zeal comes when we receive the Holy Ghost. The energy spent as a result of this great zeal needs direction. The harnessing of rivers brings enormous supplies of electricity to benefit major industries and homes. In general, the energy expended by children playing does wonder when that same energy is put to work accomplishing practical tasks. Albeit, many unwise projects launched in the name of the Lord, are of misdirected zeal. "My people are destroyed for the lack of knowledge: because thou hast rejected knowledge, I will also reject thee, that thou shalt be no priest to me: seeing thou hast forgotten the law of thy God, I will also forget thy children" (Hosea 4:6). Specific praying directed by the Holy Ghost is beneficial. What God says to man and does for man in the present is no more than a particular application of what He said to the world and did for the world once for all through the man Jesus Christ.

It is God speaking in Christ, and God's Word spoken through Christ, that is ultimately authoritative; it is the Bible that bears trustworthy witness to the speaking of that word; and it is the Holy Spirit who, in every age, mediates that authoritative word to the individual Christian and the Church (Packer 1958, 46)[16]. Moreover, praying in the Holy Ghost moves spiritual mountains out of our path and helps keep us on the straight and narrow way. One of the many works of the Holy Ghost is to help our infirmities. At the same instance, the Spirit searches our hearts – He conveys the mind of Christ. His inward work, we are brought to unity with the will of God, and this is through our praying in the Holy Ghost. Present in the teachings of Jesus is incredible promises. He promised, "He that believeth on me, the works that I do shall he also do; and greater works than these shall he do; because I go unto my Father" (John 14:12). This promise should inflame a passion in us to pray. How much self-denying must we do to become emptied to ourselves? Have we ever prayed a prayer of any length that contained no selfish expressions of our desires and wishes? Needs have never been higher than right now. Jesus

---

[16] J. I. Packer. *Fundamentalism and the Word of God: Some Evangelical Principles.* Grand Rapids, Michigan. Willian B. Eerdmans Publishing Company. 1958. Pg. 46.

said, "Whatsoever ye shall ask in my name, that will I do, that the Father may be glorified in the Son" (John 14:13). Would an answer to our prayers accentuate the beautiful revelation of God in Christ? Does the answer to our prayers emphasize and further the kingdom of God in the hearts of humanity? Or would it help our cause?

The Gospel of our Lord is designed that no flesh should glory in the presence of God. Jesus also said, "If you abide in Me, and My words abide in you, ye shall ask what ye will, it shall be done unto you" (John 15:7). Based on Stephen and Alex Kendrick in their book "*The Battle Plan for Prayer: From Basic Training to Targeted Strategies,* "Some people claim that God allows us to only ask for what we need, but never what we want. Sounds devoted and honorable, but it's not biblical. The truth is, "what ye will / whatsoever" offer runs throughout the New Testament. It's not just an isolated statement." For example, "What things so ever ye desire, when pray, believe that ye receive them, and ye shall have them" (Mark 11:24). "Whatsoever we ask, we receive of him, because we keep his commandments, and do those things please in his sight" (1 John 3:22). "If we know the he hears us, whatsoever we ask, we know that we have the petition that we desired of him" (1 John5:15). There is a noticeable pattern in the New Testament – a whatsoever pattern from God.

Prayer is designed to honor God and to meet the needs of His cause. We must strive to reach that place where what we ask in Jesus' name is granted. When we pray with faith in complete harmony with His will – God will always answer. There is such little peace and tranquility in a world where a hurting society cries out in desperation. A large segment of our society regularly resorts to tranquilizers and false hopes to escape the pressures of turmoil and conflict. All the while, the Prince of Peace is ignored in just about every facet of life. A person will never have peace until he turns to Jesus in prayer. Instead of a raging storm within, we can entertain the giver of peace. The Holy Ghost is the Comforter who brings peace to our troubled minds. Apostle Paul said in his salutation to the Corinthian church, "Finally brethren, farewell. Be perfect, be of good comfort, be of one mind, live in peace; and the God of love and peace shall be with you" (2 Corinthians 13:11). When apostle Paul tells us to agree, he is telling us to find Christ in our midst. Telling us to mend our ways means to follow Christ in our midst. Encouraging means to help each other recognize Him. Thus, to live in peace means to live with God, for God in His Son, Jesus, is our peace (Cameron 1991, 169)[17]. Jesus said, "Peace I leave with you, my peace I give you; not as the world giveth, give I unto you. Let not your heart be trouble, neither let it be afraid" (John 14:27)

Power of Prayer

It has been said, "Many people of this world will never know what prayer can do." Luke chapter 18 contains an account of five prayers that were answered, and two that were not. The reason for unanswered prayers was apparent. They were prayed from proud hearts filled with judgment toward others. They trusted in their good works for the answer instead of God's mercy. The Pharisee portrays self-righteousness. The rich young ruler represents those who hold fast to earthly possessions while asking favors of God. The prayers that were answered teaches us that prayers of importunity, when prayed in the will of God, will be answered. "If I regard iniquity in my heart, the Lord will not hear me" (Psalm 66:18). Heart cleansing is a vital part of praying effectively. The effectual prayer is the power that once closed the heavens that it did not rain three and a half years. Then the prophet Elijah prayed again, and it rained freely. Prayer has won battles that would have been lost. We have access to all the power of God through the power of prayer. However, much help is needed is at our disposal. Lord, teach us to pray!

Much has been said about non-conformity in our present time. The original nonconformists were the apostles of the first-century church. They refused to be pressed into the mold of religions of their day – they were transformed by the renewal of their mind. In a day when charismatic renewal is widespread – renewing of the mind is what God demands. As a person presents himself to God in prayer, great things are accomplished. Not only does God answer our prayers, but He also changes our attitudes. The hard Spirit of lust is dissolved and giving way to a soft, broken, and contrite sprite. For instance, when the prophet Nathan confronted David

---

[17] Peter John Cameron, Father, O.P. *Praying with Saint Paul: Daily Reflections on the Letters of the Apostle Paul.* Washington, DC. Magnificat Central Team, Inc. 1991. Pg. 169

with his sin, David accepted responsibility – he blamed no one else for his crime. Convicted by the guilt of his wrongdoing – he prayed for mercy. After repenting – thoroughly confessing his sins, he prayed to be purged. David's prayer and cry, "Restore unto me the joy of thy salvation; and uphold me with thy free spirit" (Psalm 51:12), was regarded by the Lord, and He granted him full restoration. If something has been lost in our experience, the place of renewal is in prayer.

Deliverance from all forms of bondage is ours through the Holy Ghost. Drugs, alcohol, and tobacco have been overcome through the power of God. The blood has broken the mental and religious tyranny of Jesus Christ. Often though, Satan, by his cunning devices, brings liberated souls back into bondage. Every soul void of joy, bound by thoughts contrary to godliness and defeated in Spirit, can proclaim their liberty in Jesus' name! "Stand fast therefore in the liberty wherewith Christ hath made us free, and be not entangled again with the yoke of bondage" (Galatians 5:1). In the course of life, we are thrust into a situation that is not to our enjoyment. Without pandering to disaster, circumstances press us out of shape. However, the deliverance provided by God is astounding. Daniel had a consistent, dedicated prayer life before his experience in the lions' den. There was no wavering on his part when the showdown came. Likewise, the three Hebrew young men showed unshaken confidence in their God. When offered a second chance to bow before the image of gold, they quickly responded, "If it be so, our God whom we serve is able to deliver us from the burning fiery furnace, and he will deliver us out of thine hand, O king. But if not, be it known unto thee, O king, that we will not serve thy gods, nor worship the golden image which thou hast set up" (Daniel 3:17-18). They did not know for sure that God would deliver, but they would not become idolaters in any event.

CHAPTER 5

Faithful and Loyal to God

Daniel Tested

Nothing is considered safe until it has been tested. This statement increases invalidity as the thing tested increases in importance. We may not spend much time examining the clothesline's strength, but we want to be sure the bridges we drive over will take a lot of stress. We may not test the accuracy of a yardstick if we measure cloth for a dress, but we want to be sure the instrument is exact if we are building a wing for an airplane. There is no way to know the strength or ability without testing. We may imagine our ability to lift two hundred pounds, but there is no way to know until we attempt picking up that amount of weight to test our strength. The same is true with our faith. We may claim to have faith to move mountains, but our faith is only guesswork until confronted with a mountain. James told us to rejoice when our faith is tried, "My brethren, count it all joy when ye fall into divers temptations; knowing this, that the trying of your faith worketh patience. But let patience have her perfect work, that ye may be perfect and entire, wanting nothing" (James 1:2-4). God desired to prove the quality of Daniel. If he were not genuine, it would have shown up. His spiritual strength could only be determined by examination and trial. Trouble can be a test of character; luxury may also be. Daniel went through both, and he proved to be faithful to God.

Daniel was a young man, probably about fifteen years of age, when he arrived in Babylon. He was a talented youth. Ashpenaz had been asked to seek out those who were "skillful in all wisdom, cunning in knowledge, and understanding in science, and such as ability in them to stand in the king's palace, and whom they might teach the learning and tongue of the Chaldeans" (Daniel 1:4). According to Daniel 3:1, Daniel was from a royal family in his home back in Israel, and he had everything going for him.

He could look forward to a bright future. However, suddenly there was a change in circumstance – he became a captive of a pagan king. Daniel faced a different culture in a land that did not know the true and living God. In secular measurement, the Babylonians were far advanced beyond the lowly Israelites. Daniel faced a residence foreign to his lifestyle. He could not make daily visits to the Temple to worship Jehovah. There is even the possibility that Daniel was made a eunuch, for over him was Ashpenaz, the master of the king's eunuchs. Also, he was in the king's palace in a position that would be well filled by a eunuch. To emphasize, we have no record of any marriage. However, all these circumstances would make some men rebellious. Another critical point, Daniel had a good record with both God and man. It is clear why both God and man wanted to advance him. Daniel is a young man who can be trusted, dependable, and learn to cope with any situation.

Daniel knew why he was being fattened and groomed. Daniel's ministry was unique. King Nebuchadnezzar deported him to Babylon around 605 B. C. There, and he enjoyed an education to prepare him for statecraft. Daniel's natural gifts and unique and divine endowment gave him immediate recognition as the spokesman for the Lord, the God of heaven (VanGemeren, The Progress of Redemption 2000, 277)[18]. The king of Babylon would want the young men to advance in his kingdom. In politics, it is always hard to remain honest; it is easy to compromise. The mind easily justifies the immorality, the injustice, and the competition involved in advancement.

Yet, Daniel retained his integrity. Many years later, he was still opening his window toward Jerusalem to pray. He kept up a faithful devotion to God all his life. Praying three-time times a day, he probably accumulated a record of some 75,000 prayer times with God from that window. Daniel had to live daily with the pressures from the position in the royal palace. These pressures could have been logically faced with human thinking. However, he knew the deceitfulness of the carnal mind. Nevertheless, Daniel kept turning to God. It is doubtful that he ever made any significant decisions without consulting with God and His Word. On the contrary, King Saul had failed this test many years before. Although he was a very

[18] Willem Vangemeren. *The Progress of Redemption: The Story of Salvation from Creation to the New Jerusalem.* Grand Rapids, Michigan. Baker Books. 2000. Pg. 277.

humble man initially, his pride deceived him in his royal office. He became jealous of anyone who would appear to outshine him. This is the reason for his resentment and eventual bitter hatred toward David. After one of the significant battles, the young ladies had sung, "Saul hath slain his thousands, and David his ten thousand" (I Samuel 18:7). Saul's arrogance began at that point. We read the heart of an ambitious man is in words, "What can he have more but the kingdom?" (I Samuel 18:8).

Daniel's Loyalty

We need more examples like Daniel, who remained faithful to a cause when the majority abandoned it. Daniel joined the ranks of men like Joshua and Caleb, who stood alone against popular opinion. When men stand in times like this, we know they have strong convictions with God. It is not a theory with them. May God gives us convictions to live by so that, should the time of testing or trial come, we can live and die by them. The Bible states God knows how to "frustrateth the tokens of the liars, and maketh diviners mad; that turneth wise men backward, and maketh their knowledge foolish; that confirmeth the word of his servant, and performeth the counsel of his messengers" (Isaiah 44:25-26). That is why God needs loyal men to represent His cause – they may be knowledgeable men like Daniel, uneducated men like Amos, or even an insecure leader like Gideon. Regardless, in God's hand, these loyal men can be victorious. "But God hath chosen the foolish things of the world to confound the wise, and God hath chosen the week things of the world to confound the things which are mighty; and the base things of the world, and the things which are despised, hath God has chosen, yea, and things which are not, to bring to naught the things that are" (1 Corinthians 1:27-28).

The Israelites were God's people. According to the Bible, they had been set aside as God's special people, "Now, therefore, if ye will obey my voice indeed, and keep my covenant, then ye shall be a peculiar treasure unto me above all people: for all the earth is mine" (Exodus 19:5). Therefore, Daniel could not be a dishonor to such great people. His parents had raised him to know the God of Abraham, Isaac, and Jacob. These great patriots have been world-renowned as the people of one God. It is essential to remember our heritage. We should be grateful if we were raised in the church and if our parents were godly men and women. Now, we are challenged to remain loyal to those who have established this great message of hope. Moreover, honor and respect are due to those who have paid such a huge sacrifice to see us have what we have today. Many of the early pastors may have appeared improper, and they may have been unlearned men with little financial accumulation, but we will have to work hard to have the spiritual results of their labor and anointing. Albeit, Daniel would not allow those who were not living up to Israel's name to influence him. He would be one to stand alone if need be so that the world would know why he was named "a prince of God."

Daniel's loyalty to God kept him from the king's meat, kept him praying, and made him honest and faithful to His Word. It is quite possible that others felt as if God had forsaken them at that time during the captivity. Those who overpowered them had strange gods. There was no apparent ability of Israel's God to show Himself superior to the gods of the Babylonians. The pressure allows us to offer our loyalty to the greater One. When all is going well in our lives – it is easy to be loyal. When situations are difficult, it takes a faithful person to show loyalty. Moreover, Daniel was willing to stand with God – even when He was not showing Himself strong in the midst of strange gods. Until God's miracles worked with Daniel and his three friends, the Babylonians could look upon the God of Israel with disregard. Yet, when God was being mocked during this time, there was a man who remained loyal to his cause. Many times, we can point to times and places where God has done great things. We can relate to spectacular healings and remarkable deliverances by the Lord. But suppose there are times when we pray, and there appears to be no answer. Suppose someone dies that we were sure would be healed. Even then, we can still retain our confidence in God. We know He could answer and will as we continue to believe Him. We know He can heal. We know there is nothing too hard for our God. God is not interested in fair-weather friends – He needs men and women like Daniel, who will remain loyal to Him despite the circumstances.

There is a close correlation between Daniel's people, God, and training. Israel was the recipient of the covenants of promise. They had a rich heritage in the issues as it pertains the only true God. It was in this heritage and by God-fearing parents that Daniel had obtained his early training. From a child, he had been taught the Word of God, and before he could speak, the Scriptures were read to him. He had been involved in religious ceremonies before he was capable of understanding their meaning. Based on the Jewish tradition, Daniel learned the Ten Commandments at an early age. He learned to attend the Temple service and knew the importance of sacrifice. From what the Scriptures reveal of his attitude toward God, we know his training had been well received. He had responded in the way his parents desired and, in a way, with which God was well-pleased. Daniel was trained in the form of God, for when he grew up and was carried to Babylon, the problems he faced caused him to grow in the integrity of God's Word rather than react as the world does. If we want people to continue in their loyalty to God, they must be trained to know God. They must know who He is and what He requires of His people. It is becoming apparent that we must study God's Word and become well-trained in His principles if we are going to cope with this deteriorating generation.

Daniel's Reward for Faithfulness

Much time is usually involved in rewarding men for good character traits. Seldom is there an immediate reward when one does a good deed. But eventually, it pays to retain our integrity. Daniel had remained faithful to God, justifying His ways and defending any opposition and criticism to His Word. Now God was ready to advance him for his loyalty. God was pleased with his faithfulness. In Paul's statement, "Be not deceived; God is not mocked; for whatsoever a man soweth, that shall he also reap" (Galatians 6:7), may be used for good things as well as for evil. We tend to immediately think of the mistakes that must be reaped when we read Galatians 6:7-8. However, when we have been faithful to God, we will be rewarded with favor from God. His rewarding is more lasting and more productive than reaping evil. Many people fail because they cannot wait for the heavenly reward.

Daniel's appearance made him more acceptable to those who looked on the outward man. His knowledge and wisdom were his keys to the king's court. The king of Babylon wanted those who could enhance his administration. Due to Daniel's loyalty and faithfulness to God, he excelled in all the examined areas. None of those things did he acquire by his efforts; he developed what God gave him. He indeed must have applied himself because he became ten times better than the others. This was not a man-acquired achievement – it was God's reward to him. Indeed, others would probably not have recognized Daniel's exceptional knowledge and abilities as of supernatural origin, but God does give us our intelligence. Daniel understood this when he told Nebuchadnezzar this information about God: "And he changeth the times and the seasons: he removeth kings, and sitteth up kings: he giveth wisdom unto the wise, and knowledge to them that know understanding" (Daniel 2:21). When we remain faithful to God, He always enhances the talents we already have and reveals other things that we could not have obtained otherwise. Additionally, God added even more to Daniel, such as the ability to understand dreams and visions. He would not have given this ability to Daniel except for the work He would do in Babylon.

It was through God that Daniel advanced in the Kingdom of Babylon. King Nebuchadnezzar had a dream of an image that was made of different metals. However, when he awoke, he forgot what the dream was about. Without success, he demanded of the astrologers and magicians to give their interpretation of his dream. They could not tell him what he dreamed, nor did they know what the dream meant. Specifically, this allowed Daniel to show the king that God reigns in the universe. King Nebuchadnezzar "made Daniel a great man, gave him many great gifts, and made him ruler over the whole province of Babylon, and chief of the governors over all the wise men of Babylon" (Daniel 2:48). By Daniel's influence in the kingdom, he was also able to promote his three friends. "Then Daniel requested of the king, and he set Sha-drach, Me-shach, and Abed-nego, over the affairs of the province Babylon: but Daniel sat in the gate of the king" (Daniel 2:49). When God determines to promote someone, it is incredible how he can put the right circumstance together. Daniel's significance should be noted in that when new kings reigned, and new nations ruled, he remained in high positions. Such men were often discarded, if not killed by the new kings, to be replaced by those more suitable to the new king's taste. However, when Darius, the Median king who had conquered Babylon, decided to choose three presidents, Daniel was made first of the three. "Then this Daniel was preferred above the presidents and princes because an excellent spirit was in him, and the king thought to set him over the whole realm.

CHAPTER 6

The Christian and Three Vital Factors

The Christian and Prayer

Sometimes just the mention of prayer sends guilt feeling creeping down the spiritual spine. Unfortunately, most of the time, prayer is something we talk about more than something we do. Perhaps no other Christian discipline is so firmly believed, yet prayer time often ends up at the bottom of a person's priority list. A desire to pray must come from a desire to be like Jesus and to have fellowship with Him. If prayer is just a cold ritual achieved through self-discipline, our prayer will be a powerless drudgery. If we only pray when in need, our prayers will be sporadic, and when rare an event takes place, it will be a session of begging. If we pray when we only feel a great inspiration, our prayers will be extraordinary indeed. The disciples felt a desire to pray when they heard and saw Jesus in prayer – they were inspired to pray like Him (Ladd 1993, 237)[19]. They asked a question that revealed their feeling of inadequacy, yet a strong desire to pray: "Lord, teach us to pray" (Luke 11:1). The first phase of developing a productive prayer life is to have a desire! If we seek God for instruction and inspiration in prayer – we will grow in our effectiveness.

Jesus mastered the divine art of prayer, and He left us with many beautiful examples of prayer. First of all, Jesus prayed before making a spiritual decision. "He went out into a mountain to pray and continued all night in prayer to God. And when it was day, he called unto him his disciples: and of them, he chose twelve" (Luke 6:12-13). Secondly, prayer is more important to Christ than social life. "And when he had sent the multitudes away, he went up into a mountain apart to pray: and when evening was come, he was there alone" (Matthew 14:23). Thirdly, prayer

---

[19] George Eldon Ladd. *A Theology of the New Testament.* Grand Rapids, Michigan. William B. Eerdmans Publishing Company. 1993. Pg. 237.

was first on Jesus' schedule. "And in the morning, rising up a great while before day, he went out, and departed into a solitary place, and there prayed" (Mark 1:35). Lastly, Jesus prayed in times of crisis. "And being in an agony he prayed more earnestly: and his sweat was as it were great drops of blood falling to the ground" (Luke 22:44). Now, why was it so important to us that Jesus prayed? The Bible says, "For even hereunto were ye called; because Christ also suffered for us, leaving us an example, that ye should follow his steps" (1 Peter 2:21). Jesus said, "For I have given you an example, that ye should do as I have done to you" (John 13:15). Jesus has provided a great example of the need for the power of prayer. The discipline of prayer forms one of the fundamental aspects of spiritual development and usefulness in the kingdom of God.

Prayer is an essential part of the Christian life. The following topics illustrate the essential element of prayer in the Christian life: a) Every person who is born again first prays the prayer of repentance, b) Prayer is necessary for a continual communion with God, c) The Christian's life is filled with thanksgiving, praise, and worship, and these are aspects of prayer, d) Prayer is a source of spiritual strength (Matthew 26:41), f) Prayer releases God's power to work miracles in our lives (Psalm 91:15; John 15:7), and g) Prayer is an excellent method of expressing faith in God - it verbalizes our faith. In prayer, we are assisted by the Holy Ghost to believe even more substantial. Considering the excellent benefit of prayer and the definite biblical instructions to pray, it seems obvious prayer should be practiced daily. Prayer is not only a benefit, but it is also a requirement, for, without its application, we are cut off from the Source of life, light, and love. No one can read the gospels and fail to realize that Christ continuously urged His followers to make it the important business of their lives to pray. From Christ's example, we learn the necessity of prayer (Lockyer 1964, 225)[20].

---

[20] Herbert Lockyer. *All the Doctrines of the Bible*. Grand Rapids, Michigan. Zondervan Publishing. 1964. Pg. 225.

The Christian and God's Word

The Bible is a unique book in the world. If a person stacked all the books in the world – forming a giant mountain of books, the Bible would be higher than them all. The Bible is a particular Book having many unique characteristics. The following are details about the Bible: a) The Bible was written over 1,600 years (sixty generations), b) forty or more authors wrote the Bible from a variety of backgrounds, c) The Bible was written on three continents: Africa, Asia, and Europe, d) The Bible was written in three languages: Hebrew, Aramaic, and Greek, e) The Bible deals with hundreds of controversial subjects, yet there is comprehensive agreement throughout, f) The Bible has been read by more people and published in more languages than any other book, g) The Bible was preserved by scribes who practiced almost perfect fidelity in the transcribing of the Bible for posterity, resulting in excellent retention of accuracy, h) The Bible has proven over and over its historical accuracy as a reliable source of Hebrew history, unequaled in the world (Lohse 1985, 191)[21], and i) Hundreds of ancient Bible prophecies have been fulfilled in history. The unique quality of the Bible is its divine inspiration. "For the prophecy came not in the old time by the will of man: but holy men of God spake as they were moved by the Holy Ghost" (2 Peter 1:21). It is God's Word to man – forming the Christian's sole foundation of faith. The Bible is the standard by which all truth is measured.

The Word of God is the means through which God reveals Himself to humanity. Therefore, there is great value in reading the Bible. The longest Psalm is Psalm 119; it is given entirely to the subject of the Word of God. The psalmist emphasized that inspiration, instruction, and spiritual food are found in the Scriptures. For this reason, daily Bible reading is a great discipline. God will send His Holy Spirit to assist the reader in the comprehension of His Word. However, reading the Bible can be a real challenge in our contemporary society. Today, there is so much colorful visual imagery to stimulate our senses through magazines, pictorial books, and novels. There is an abundance of easy-to-read, entertaining material available today, which will easily take our minds off the Bible. Nevertheless,

---

[21] Bernhard Lohse. *A Short History of Christian Doctrine: From the First Century to the Present.* Philadelphia, PA. Fortress Press. 1985. Pg. 191.

every Christian should seek to read the Bible through each year; reading a few chapters each day will accomplish this goal. Reading the Bible gives us a sense of accomplishment from cover to cover in a specific frame! The Word of God will be hidden away in our hearts for special times of need. The more we read the Bible – the more exciting and fruitful our reading becomes. It is spiritual food to the Spirit of man, making him steadfast in the faith.

The richness of the Word of God makes it the kind of reading that requires slow, deep meditation. Speed reading may be beneficial for specific material types, but it is not very practical when reading the Bible. Great emphasis was put upon the Scriptures by the Hebrews. Under the leadership of Moses, the Lord gave them firm instructions to love and study the Law. For the Word of the Lord says, "And these words, which I command thee this day, shall be in thine heart: And thou shalt teach them diligently unto thy children, and shalt talk of them when thou sittest in thine house, and when thou walkest by the way, and when thou risest up. And thou shalt bind them for a sign upon thine hand, and they shall be as frontlets between thine eyes. And thou shalt write them upon the post of thy house, and on thy gates" (Deuteronomy 6:6-9). In the New Testament, the Bereans are commended for their study of the Scriptures. Luke recorded that they searched the scriptures daily, and as a result, high numbers came to know the Lord. For the Scriptures states: "And the brethren immediately sent away Paul and Silas by night unto Berea: Who coming thither went into the synagogue of the Jews. These were nobler than those in Thessalonica, in that they received the Word with all readiness of mind, and searched the scriptures daily, whether those things were so. Therefore, many of them believed; also, of honorable women which were Greeks, and of men, not a few" (Acts 17:10-12). Additionally, studying the Bible produces faith. It is a source of daily spiritual food, and it is a great inspiration to the Spirit of man.

The Bible is our offensive weapon and revealer of God's power. "the sword of the Spirit, which is the word of God" (Ephesian 6:17). It is evident that the Bible is not to be the glamorous decoration of God's color guard, nor is it treated as some spiritual relic and kept in the musty archives. It is a weapon to be used in the heat of the battle to inflict the mortal blow against our spiritual enemy. God's Word is a weapon used against Satan amid temptation (Matthew 4:1-11). It is a great weapon to stop the mouth of the gainsayer (Titus 1:9). The Word of God is also a great weapon to convert hungry hearts to salvation in Jesus Christ, which strikes at the very heart of man's enemy, Satan himself. One of the most important uses of the Word of God is for witnessing. Apollos, from Alexandria, was an eloquent man and mighty in the Scriptures. He was in Ephesus preaching John's Baptism, for this was all the truth he knew at the time. Aquila and Priscilla called him aside, and however, "expounded unto him the way of God more perfectly." Apollos was converted and went forth "shewing by the scriptures that Jesus was Christ" (Acts 18:24-28). God's Word was the weapon that brought about Apollos' conversion and the cause for the revival that followed him becoming a Christian.

The Christian and the Spirit

After His resurrection, Jesus urged his disciples to receive the Spirit. The Bible states, "And when he had said this, he breathed on them, and saith unto them, Receive ye the Holy Ghost" (John 20:22). Jesus commissioned them to experience the new birth and go into all the world and preach the kingdom. Jesus knew they would need extraordinary power to continue the work He had started, so He breathed on them, symbolizing that the Holy Ghost would be His very presence with them (Clark 1990, 227)[22]. The disciples did not receive the Holy Ghost on this occasion, for the Holy Ghost was not yet poured out. It was not until fifty days later in an upper room, on the Day of Pentecost, that the Holy Ghost was poured out - fulfilling the promise of Jesus as told in (Acts 2:1-4). According to Donald Guthrie in his book on page 528, *"New Testament Theology,"* he also promised the Holy Ghost would be a power source. "Although in Luke's account of Jesus' farewell words (Luke 24:49), no mention is made of the Spirit, the words "stay in the city of Jerusalem, until ye be endued with power from on high," taken in conjunction with Luke's second volume, clearly refers to the descent of Spirit of Pentecost."

Receiving the Holy Ghost, with evidence of speaking with other

---

[22] David K. Clark and Norman L. Geisler. *Apologetics in the New Age: A Christian Critique of Pantheism. Eugen, Oregon.* Wipf and Stock Publishers. 1990. Pg. 227.

tongues, was a typical experience in the New Testament church. When unbelievers were converted to Christianity, they received the Holy Ghost. The following examples make it understandable that converts of the first-century church received the Holy Ghost: a) At Pentecost, they were filled with the Holy Ghost and spoke with tongues (Acts 2:4), b) In Samaria, believers received the Holy Ghost when Peter and John laid hands on then (Acts 8:14-17), c) Paul, this persecutor of Christians received the Holy Ghost when he converted to this hated new religion (Acts 9:17), e) In Caesarea, Cornelius and his household received the Holy Ghost – becoming the first Gentiles converted to Christianity (Acts 10:44-48), and f) In Ephesus, Paul preached to the twelve disciples of John the Baptist, and they received the Holy Ghost (Acts 19:1-7). Furthermore, believing the gospel message is just the initial spark of life that leads to the new-birth experience. Repentance is the experience that cleanses our life and empties our hearts of impurities. In water baptism, a person by faith buries his old nature in a watery grave. However, the infilling of the Holy Ghost is the completion of the new-birth experience. We then become a new creation in Christ Jesus, having been transformed by the power of the Holy Spirit.

Being a spiritual person is manifesting the Spirit of God in one's life. There are two ways the Spirit is manifest in a believer's presence: manifested by the gifts of Spirit and the fruit of the Spirit. "And these signs shall follow them that believe; In my name shall they cast out devils; they shall speak with new tongues; They shall take up serpents; and if drink any deadly thing, it shall not hurt them; they shall lay hands on the sick, and they shall recover" (Mark 16:17-18). The New Testament church saw the fulfillment of this promise and was much blessed with signs and wonders. "And many wonders and signs were done by the apostles" (Acts 2:43). Paul lists the gifts of the Spirit in I Corinthians 12. They are given as a manifestation of the Spirit to profit the church body, according to verse 7. We are not to be shy about the gifts of the Spirit, but we are to "desire spiritual gifts and "forbid not to speak with tongues" (I Corinthians 14:1,39). The second and most important way in which the Spirit is manifested in our lives is through the fruit of the Spirit. Many people will never read a Bible, but they will observe our Spirit-filled life and see Jesus Christ through us. "Let your light so shine before men, that they may see your good works, and glorify your Father which is in heaven" (Matthew 5:16).

CHAPTER 7

The Healing Touch

The Suffering Woman

"And a certain woman, which had an issue of blood twelve years, and had suffered many things of many physicians, and had spent all that she had, and was nothing better, but rather grew worse" (Mark 5:25-26). An unnamed suffering woman is the main character in this narrative of healing. The writer of the Scripture either did not know her name or did not reveal it – yet she suffered and continued in her agony. But when an unknown suffering woman met a well-known healing Lord, a circuit of healing connected them and allowed a dynamic flow of Christ's virtue. In electrical terms, one might say that He was connected directly to heaven's power source, and the woman was grounded; therefore, the healing current passed from Him to her. "A certain woman and "a certain man" are terms that frequently occur in the New Testament.

The terms designate unnamed characters in parables as well as actual occurrences. The words "a certain" differentiate one particular person from the rest of the crowd. A number, an unknown face in the group, an insignificant nobody – these are terms that describe how many people feel when they think about themselves and the vast number of people in the world. The world population is well over seven billion people. When one considers several such people, his or her sense of importance diminishes. If a person is tempted to feel that he does not matter because he is just one small person among the billions of the world, he should remember that Jesus sees all things and everyone. He heard the voice of the blind man above the loudness of the crowd on the Jericho road. Also, He felt the woman with the issue touch among all of the groups that brushed against him.

Unable to find a physician who could halt her illness's progress – the

47

woman both failed to improve and saw her condition worsen. "And was nothing better, but rather grew worse" (Mark 5:25). The hemorrhaging was gradually draining her life's strength. It is doubtful that she could have survived much longer. According to Leviticus 17:11, the life of the flesh is in the blood. Therefore, losing her blood meant that she was losing her life. If sickness took its toll only on the physical body - it would be bad enough. However, disease always opens the door for emotional trauma, especially if there is no improvement. Every person senses some uncertainty or fear of dying if the sickness is severe. Moreover, when that fear is accompanied by a disease that does not improve – it affects the emotions as well. Without hope or knowledge of improvement of their sickness, the person often experiences discouragement. The body is affected by disease both physically and emotionally. One common emotional side effect of illness is fear that the condition is worse than it is. Although the Bible does not give us a complete diagnosis of the woman's sickness, it is probably safe to assume that she was suffering emotional distress along with her physical affliction. It would be impossible to suffer as she suffered for twelve years and not be affected emotionally.

When a sick person goes to a doctor who cannot help her, she usually seeks help from another doctor. She may even visit another doctor to get a second opinion. It can be very frustrating when she cannot find a physician that can help Her. Such was the predicament of the woman who had suffered for twelve long years. The Word of God says that she "suffered many things of many physicians," but we do not know how many. Whatever the number, it was too many for the languishing woman. She seemed to be near the end of her physical and mental endurance. Notwithstanding, physicians are supposed to contribute to the improvement of a patient's condition. How unfortunate when they contribute to the deterioration of the patient's condition. It was enough to suffer from her illness, but she also experienced many things from many physicians. The Bible goes on to say the suffering woman spent all but suffered even more, "And had suffered many things of many physicians, and had spent all that she had, and was nothing bettered, but rather grew worse" (Mark 5:26) (McWilliams 2006, 71,150)[23]. The woman's spending and her suffering continued with both

[23] Warren McWilliams. *Where is the God of Justice? Bible Perspectives on Suffering.* Peabody, Massachusetts. Hendrickson Publishers. Inc. 2006. Pg. 71, 150.

spiraling upward. As her misery increased, her money decreased until she had nothing but pain. She was proof that compensation cannot always buy comfort - how exhausting to the body and emotions when, in addition to the sickness, one's finances are diminished. Having spent all, she had no more resources with which to seek help.

In Need of a Touch

"When she had heard of Jesus, came in the press behind, and touched his garment" (Mark 5:27). When the suffering woman heard of Jesus, she believed that she would be healed if she could get to Him and touch His garment. The message of hope is like a light in the night of hopelessness. When no one can help and a ray of hope shines through all the fog of despair, it represents the dawning of a new day. To the suffering woman, the reports of a healer and the possibility that she could get to Him transformed her night of need into an hour of hope. Her hope then became faith. "So, then faith cometh by hearing and hearing by the word of God" (Romans 10:17). Additionally, she heard, and she believed. The woman with the issue of blood was heard, but there were many sick people in Jesus' day that never listened to the message of hope that brought her to Jesus. Furthermore, there are many people today who have not heard.

The woman did not just hear and hope, but she acted upon her hope by going to Jesus. Her going, however, was not without difficulty. She had to get through a great crowd to get to Jesus. The Bible says, "Much people followed him, and thronged him" (Mark 5:24). Also, the Bible called the crowd "the press." Despite the impediment, she began to make her way to Jesus. Her faith caused her to act. She "came in the press behind." Whether she anticipated less resistance in getting to Jesus or whether she felt unworthy to approach Him from the front, we do not know. However, we know that she was able to overcome all the hindrances between Jesus and her. The biblical narrative sequences the woman's success in obtaining her healing as follows: a) the voice of faith, b) the effort of faith, and c) the touch of Jesus' garment. If she had exerted effort without faith, there would have been no healing. Nevertheless, she believed and moved to touch His garment. In general, too many people depend only on faith. James asked a rhetorical question: "What doth it profit, my brethren, though a man say he hath faith, and have not works? Can faith save him?" (James 2:14). Of course, the answer is no; James explained that we must have works with our faith. Although it is impossible to please God without faith, neither can faith without works, please Him. James said that faith without works is dead (James 2:26).

"And straightway the fountain of her blood dried up, and she felt in her body that she was healed of that plague" (Mark 5:29). The suffering woman was healed immediately. She did not have to wait several days or weeks to receive her miracle – the healing in her body was immediate. Jesus dried up the fountain of blood, and she was healed within minutes. Jesus both healed her immediately and did so without charge. She finally could be free from pain and suffering because of His grace, love, and mercy. Luke 8:44 records that "immediately her issue of blood stanched." The word stanched means "to stand still." When she touched Jesus, and His virtue touched her, the flowing blooding ceased at once. Indeed, Jesus can stop things that no one else can control, and He can start something that no one else can begin. The Bible record many beautiful examples of this. For instance, when the Israelites were on their way to Canaan, and the priests stepped into the Jordan River – the flowing river could no longer flow (Joshua 3:15-17). Joshua 3:15 says it was during harvest, a period of the year known for flooding. Yet God stopped the flow of the river for His people to pass over. Another excellent example is that Lazarus had been dead for four days when Jesus called him from the tomb and restored life to him. What more perfect illustration of Christ's power could there be? All authority in heaven and earth belongs to Him.

Touching Jesus

The suffering woman touched Jesus, believing that she would be healed. She was influenced by a strong determination to reach the One who could help with the significant issue that plagued her. Having suffered for twelve years, maybe her healing was all she could think about and hope for. Her desperation drove her to find and touch Jesus. Moreover, when faced with great hindrances in getting to him through the crowd – that same desperation gave her the courage and determination to press forward. Desperate people often find a way to get what they need. This suffering woman was no exception. There was a need so severe that it surpasses friendliness. Conceivably this is what Jesus was describing when He stated about the kingdom, "And from the days of John the Baptist until now the kingdom of heaven suffereth violence, and the violent take it by force" (Matthew 11:12).

The suffering woman made up her mind that nothing would keep her from her last resort for help. Conceivably it is difficult for us to understand what a barrier the throng represented to this sick woman. The crowd would have been demanding even for a healthy person to walk through, but she was weak from her lingering illness. For her to move through many people in her condition, she had to be extremely determined and courageous. Finally, after being shoved and shunned by the multitude, she reached her point of destination – Jesus. Now she had to have the courage to reach out and touch Him. The Bible says that virtue emanated from Jesus to the suffering woman. The attribute in Mark 5:30 is translated from the Greek word Dunamis – the name means force, incredibly miraculous power. Dunamis is the same Greek word that is translated into power in Acts 1:8. "But ye shall receive power, after that the Holy Ghost comes upon you."

"And he said unto her; Daughter; thy faith hath made thee whole; go in peace, and be whole of thy plague" (Mark 5:34). The once suffering woman's healing brought her peace. For the first time in twelve years, she was without pain. The confusion, frustration, disappointment, and failure were all gone. "Go in peace" were the most beautiful words that she had ever heard. She was whole and at peace. She had known enough of a miserable existence and was ready for order in her life. His touch, whether for healing, salvation, or deliverance, always brings peace. However, Jesus' peace is of such quality that there is no global peace that compares with it. He said, "Peace I leave with you, my peace I give unto you: not as the world giveth, give I unto you" (John 14:27). The woman with the issue of blood is touching Jesus Christ with her faith, and consequently, she was healed. She believed that she would be relieved when she feels Him, and she was!

CHAPTER 8

Trusting the Master

Prayer Request

Mark 4:35-5:43 contains some of the most remarkable events in the earthly ministry of Jesus Christ. Jesus and His disciples were traveling by ship from Capernaum to the country of the Gadarenes. When their boat was caught in a violent storm – the Lord suppressed the wind and the waves with a single command. In Mark 5:1-20, the small crew met the demoniac Legion. Jesus demanded that the evil spirits leave the tormented man, and "the unclean spirits went out" (Mark 5:13). Neither a storm produced by nature nor a thunderstorm produced by demons was capable of resisting the power of the Lord. Jesus Christ still meets the greatest needs of humanity. He is still capable of setting us free from sickness and death – the dreaded by-products of sins. The Bible reveals that Jairus had observed the worsening condition of his twelve-year-old daughter. His only child's critical illness had become life-threatening. Conceivably, the synagogue ruler had first become worried, then extremely alarmed, as he viewed his daughter's condition. As time passed, probably her complexion had grown paler, and her breathing became more difficult. Like a deadly intruder, death had moved into the room, and Jairus felt its shadow across the lives of both him and the child's mother.

It would have been strange if Jairus had not heard and maybe seen much of the healing ministry of Jesus from Nazareth. Jesus had made His headquarters in Capernaum - the Lord often taught in that city. News now reached the ruler, as it had reached many, that Jesus had returned by boat to Capernaum. As Jairus hurried toward the shoreline of the Sea of Galilee, probably at this point, his thoughts must have been racing. A great crowd of people had already gathered to greet the Lord, "And it came to pass, that, when Jesus was returned, the people gladly received him: for they were all waiting for him" (Luke 8:40). Some were ill and feeble, but no one felt a greater urgency to see Jesus than this father with a dying daughter. If there was a probability for his girl at all, he knew it lay in reaching the Lord. Jairus had left the place of death to find a place of life. He left a home of despair to find a place of hope. Possibly in the past, Jairus had seen the Lord touch and heal others. He may have seen the disabled people walk. He may have witnessed lepers healed. It must have all seemed refreshing to see what Jesus did for the unfortunates. Now, however, Jairus stood in tremendous need himself. If only there would-be time for Jesus to come to his home!

"And when he saw him, he fell at his feet" (Mark 5:22). At this critical moment, Jairus threw himself down before the Lord. Yes, this was an act of desperation; what and the ruler did exceptionally. But Jairus had an urgent need. At Sychar, the Samaritan woman had left her water jar behind after meeting Jesus. Near Jericho blind, Bartimaeus threw off his beggar's garment. Here, on the dusty streets of Capernaum, a respected religious ruler cast away his pride. If prostrating himself before the Lord would help, then Jairus would willingly humble himself at the feet of the traveling preacher. In the Gospel of Matthew, the Scripture reveals, "While he spake these things unto them, behold, there came a certain ruler, and worshipped him, saying, my daughter is even now dead: but come and lay thy hand upon her, and she shall live" (Matthew 9:18). Jairus approached the Lord with the right attitude. By offering adoration and praise to Christ, Jairus acknowledged His greatness. The ruler's worship went beyond pure formality; however, it expressed faith and confidence in the Savior's power to heal and deliver. Worship lifts our spirit to God - it is a transforming experience. We are changed as we exalt the Lord for who He is and not only for what He may do for us. There were many townspeople near Jesus on the shore that day, but the desperate cry of Jairus caught Christ's attention. The ruler pleaded that the Lord would come and touch his daughter. "And besought him greatly saying, my little daughter lieth at the point of death: I pray thee, come and lay thy hands on her, that she may be healed; and she shall live" (Mark 5:23).

Many believers can relate to the fact that coming to Jesus is a humbling experience. Initially, many felt that going to an altar was an admission of guilt, and actually, it was. They tried to hide their tears of shame, and some maintained their composure. However, somehow the Holy Ghost began to minister to their heart, and they found themselves weeping uncontrollably at the foot of the Cross. They had hoped to escape God's presence unnoticed, but conviction took hold on their hearts that they could no longer hide their sins. According to the word of God, sinners are continually stumbling and falling. "From the sole even unto the head there is no soundness in it; but wounds, and bruises, putrefying sores: they have not closed, neither bound up, neither mollified with ointment" (Isaiah 1:6). "The way of the wicked is as darkness: they know not at what they stumble" (Proverbs 4:19). It often seems that they have tried everything else but Jesus, and everything else has failed. Their wounds "have not been closed, neither bound up, neither mollified with ointment" (Isaiah 1;6). Indeed, there is an ointment for healing wounds, a balm in Gilead. Many have discovered the Great Physician. They may have thought their case was hopeless, as the man on the road to Jericho – he had been stripped, wounded, and left half dead by his enemy. Then one came to pour in oil and wine in his wounds. Though he was a stranger, he was full of compassion. To His critics, Jesus replied, "They that are whole need not a physician, but they that are sick. I came not to call the righteous, but sinners to repentance" (Luke 5:31-32). Moreover, it is far better to be broken at the feet of Jesus than to stand in one's strength! Likewise, it is far better to cry out for His healing touch than to endure sickness of the soul!

Jesus began to make His way toward the ruler's home, but the progress was painfully slow. The people followed Jesus and thronged Him; the streets were narrow, and the crowd probably jostled to get a closer look at the master. As Jairus led the way to his home, naturally, he hated the shoving crowd's delay and unruly behavior. During all the confusion, Jesus suddenly stopped. To the surprise of all, "Jesus, immediately knowing in himself that virtue had gone out of him, turned him about in the press, and said, who touched my clothes?" (Mark 5:30). "His disciples said, what are you talking about? With this crowd pushing and jostling you, you're asking, who touched me? Dozens have touched you!" (Mark 5:31, The Message, MSG). Jesus knew that amid all the brushing by the great company of people – someone had intentionally touched Him with a need. Jesus recognized that "virtue," or "healing power" had gone out from him. "According to your faith, be it unto you" were the words that Jesus spoke to the two blind men in Matthew 9:29. Everyone who will receive much from the Master needs a vigorous and expectant faith. This type of faith was expressed by the woman who touched Jesus' garment while He traveled with Jairus. She had suffered for twelve long years with chronic bleeding. But despite the embarrassment of her problem, even though she had born much through the ignorant practices of many physicians, and also though she had spent all her money – the woman had high confidence that she could do something. She had fervently believed that Jesus possessed the power to restore her health with only a simple gesture on her part. "If I may touch but his clothes," she had said "I shall be whole" (Mark 5:28).

A Word of Faith

While the woman and others listened to Christ's gracious words, the devastating news came from Jairus's home. The message was brief and unnecessarily blunt. "Thy daughter is dead: why troubles thou the Master any further?" (Mark 5:35). A storm of emotion began to break in the heart of the father. Fear sprang up, and hope vanished in a moment. It seemed he would be broken and crushed by the reality of what just happened. In life itself, the scene was one of the dramatic contrasts. Here was a ruler who had just lost a daughter of about twelve years of age. Here also was a woman who had suffered a degrading affliction for twelve years and had been marvelously healed. On one side, hope appeared to be forever lost; on the other, hope seemed suddenly reclaimed (Cobbs 2018, 32)[24]. Both Jairus and the woman had come to Jesus with exceptional needs, and both had shown an active faith in His healing power. But only the woman, at this point, seemed to have been rewarded for her faith in the Lord. Christians need to understand that God's delays are not denials. For instance, Mary and Martha thought that Jesus had come four days too late to Bethany. Strangely, the news of Lazarus' sickness had not caused the Lord to hurry home to His friends. In fact, "he abode two days still in the same place where he was" (John 11:6). Christ told His disciples that he was "glad" for their sakes that He was not at Bethany "to the intent that ye may believe"

---

[24] Elizabeth Cobbs. *Watch and Pray: How to Pray Effectively During the Eight Prayer watches.* Wheaton, IL. Christ Ministries of Canton. 2018. Pg. 32.

(John 11;15). Sometimes, God's higher purpose calls for a delay in our receiving the answers we so desperately desire.

In general, death seems so final. For many, it is the ultimate shattering of hope. It is the brutal bully that takes either the young or the old and squeezes out their last breath. It is the terrorizing thief who steals from both the rich and the poor. Ultimately, it conquers generals and overthrows great kings. On March 25, 2020, in the United States, according to the Washington Post and the MSNBC News, "today was the deadliest day yet for the United States" - the total number of confirmed cases for the coronavirus is 64,000, and the death toll is currently 840. At this point, these numbers have doubled every three days in the United States. Naturally, with the rapid spread of this virus, the fear of death has captivated the minds of many. No one could defeat death until Christ appeared, and until His resurrection, not even the disciples realized how to complete a triumph He would gain. It was the Lord Jesus, who finally answered the age-old question, "If a man dies, shall he live again" (Job 14:14). And it was the Lord Jesus who gave believers victory over death; "But thanks be to God, which giveth us the victory through our Lord Jesus Christ" (1 Corinthians 15:57). Can we imagine Jairus standing in the middle of the street that day in Capernaum? Can we imagine his inner thoughts struggling to comprehend what he had just heard? Did Jairus know what had taken place some thirty miles to the southwest? Had he heard or had he been told of the widow's son who was resurrected at Nain?

Jairus had come so far through faith in Christ. Would his trust be strong enough to carry him beyond the significant obstacle of his daughter's death? Thankfully, God never allows those who lean heavily on His Word to be pushed too far. "There hath no temptation taken you but such as is common to man: but God is faithful, who will not suffer you to be tempted above that ye are able; but will with the temptation also make a way to escape, that ye may be able to bear it" (1 Corinthians 10:13). At the most critical moment - Jesus intervened. As soon as He heard the message from the ruler's home – Christ responded. His strength reveals itself in our times of most considerable distress. There was something about the words of Christ that stirred Jairus: "Be not afraid, only believe" (Mark 5:36). Jairus had believed and had thrown himself on the compassion of the healer, and yet, Jesus was asking for something more. There was a further step that the Lord was requesting the father to take. Sometimes in a believer's experience, there is a need to have a more profound dependence upon the Almighty. Christ was taking Jairus to a new dimension of faith. The storm of fear was at its height. Reason said that all hope was gone, but Jesus said, "Only believe." Christ's command meant "be believing." The present imperative form of the verb indicates that Jairus was to keep on entrusting himself to the Lord. There must be no hesitancy and no wavering. The child was dead, but Jesus had said, "Fear not: believe only, and she shall be made whole" (Luke 8:50).

A Word of Hope

We do not know what Jairus thought at that point. We do know that he walked on in hope. Although the promise had not yet been fulfilled – the confidence of the ruler had been renewed. "Hope deferred maketh the heart sick: but when desire cometh, it is a tree of life" (Proverbs 13:12). Jairus led Jesus down the familiar street to his home. When they arrived at the house, he allowed only three disciples – Peter, James, and John to go in with Him and Jairus. There was a great commotion inside the dead girl's home. The word "tumult" in Mark 5:38 can be translated "uproar." Jesus saw "the minstrels and the people making noise" (Matthew 9:23). Flute players, pipers, and wailing mourners filled the house with awful discord. Jesus is sensitive to human grief. He is "touch with the feeling of our infirmities" (Hebrews 4:15). He wept at the tomb of His friend Lazarus. But the terrible commotion of the hired mourners was artificial and out of place. They were filled with their performance. They could not grasp the reality of what was about to happen. Christ had come to give life, and that more abundantly.

The professional mourners wailed at the top of their voices. How could Jesus try to minister in such an atmosphere? How could Jesus inspire hope and faith in the hearts of Jairus and his wife in such an environment? Everything that the mourners did was contrary to what Christ was about to do. Their cries only added to the anguish of the grieving parents. Then Jesus said something that must have startled everyone: "Why make ye this ado, and week? The damsel is not dead, but sleepeth" (Mark 5:39). The Lord knew the girl had died physically, but He spoke of her spirit sleeping.

It was only a momentary slumber for her; nothing was final about what had happened. Jesus would soon awaken the girl from her inactivity, as a father might gently awaken his child. Death was not to be feared; It was about to be conquered. Many times, in the Scriptures, the dead are spoken of as sleeping. For example, "And many of them that sleep in the dust of the earth shall awake, some to everlasting life, and some to shame and everlasting contempt" (Daniel 12;2). Also, "After that, he was seen of above five hundred brethren at once, of whom the greater part remains unto this present, but some are fallen asleep" (1 Corinthians 15:6). This also was the picture presented by the Savior for His disciples in John 11:11: "Our friend Lazarus sleepeth; but I go, that I may awake him out of sleep."

Jesus was often distraught at the lack of response of those in His home city of Nazareth and His adopted home of Capernaum. Most of His mighty works were done in Capernaum and the populated areas near the Sea of Galilee. Eventually, the Lord would rebuke the Galilean cities of Chorazin, Bethsaida, and Capernaum for their unbelief. These cities had enjoyed such privileges, and yet they were unrepentant. The Lord unfavorably compared Chorazin and Bethsaida with the pagan cities of Tyre and Sidon. He compared prosperous Capernaum to the wicked city of Sodom: "And thou, Capernaum, which art exalted unto heaven, shalt be brought down to hell: for if the mighty works, which have been done in thee, had been done in Sodom, it would have remained until this day" (Matthew 11:23). For Capernaum, the final judgment would be dreadful. That city had received great light, was all and the more responsible. The pride and self-conceit of those gathered in Jairus's home were appalling. Since their mourning was done without any real compassion – it was easy to mock this stranger who dared to question their actions. Their wailing quickly turned to laughter. How strange! They thought as they considered the words of Jesus: "And they laughed him to scorn, knowing that she was dead" (Luke 8:53).

Unbelief disqualified the mourners from seeing a marvelous miracle. If only they had believed Christ's spoken word! If only they had shown some courtesy and respect for this great One who stood among them! They could have received an abundance of blessings if they had only recognized that this was "the time when God was visiting them." The Scriptures say, "And shall lay thee even with the ground, and thy children within thee; and they shall not leave in thee one stone upon another; because thou knewest not the time of thy visitation" (Luke 19:44). But unbelief disguises itself in a garment of arrogant pride. Unbelief always excludes individuals from enjoying the promises of God. It robbed the mourners that day, for Christ put them all out of the house. A lack of faith is an active hindrance to the work of God. When Jesus was visiting in Nazareth, unbelief obstructed individuals from bringing their needs where they could be satisfied. "And he did not many mighty works there because of their unbelief" (Matthew 13:58).

A Word of Power

The Lord led the father, the mother, and His three disciples into the place where the young girl lay. As Christ took charge, everything was sure to change. Death, indeed, was rendered powerless in the presence of the Prince of life: "And killed the Prince of life, whom God hath raised from the dead; whereof we are witnesses" (Acts 3:15). Jesus, having taken the dead child by the hand, spoke an Aramaic expression, "Talitha cumi" (Mark 5:41), which meant "Little girl, I say to you, arise." How easy the Lord dealt with the situation! How quickly the transformation took place! "And straightway the damsel arose, and walked; for she was of the age of twelve years. And they were astonished by a great astonishment" (Mark 5:42). Jairus and his wife could have added more details as to what happened. They had heard Jesus' gracious command. They had seen the motionlessness of death and then the movement of life. Then, as if waking from a peaceful dream, their daughter had opened her eyes. They probably embraced their only child and felt the warmth of her cheek. Undoubtedly, their hearts overflowed with joy as they saw their daughter walking.

Jesus had conquered and overthrew death. He had driven it outside, just like the foolish mourners. There was no need for wailing now. Forget all the sad moaning and weeping. Christ had come with healing and life-restoring power. "The thief cometh not, but for to steal, and to kill, and to destroy: I have come that they might have life and that they might have it more abundantly" (John 10:10). When Jesus speaks, nature must respond to His command. A fig tree, cursed by the Lord, must wither and die at his power. Water turns to wine, and bread and fish multiply.

When the Lord speaks to the raging elements, they must obey. The sea has to become quiet, and the wind has to cease. What high power was delivered through the spoken word of the Lord Jesus! When Christ said, "Arise," a paralyzed man took up his bed and walked (Matthew 9:6-7), a leper walked away restored (Luke 17:19), and a young man rose from a funeral bier (Luke 7:14). Indeed, with Jesus, prayer was a communion point with His heavenly Father and the source of His miracle ministry. Jesus demonstrated a lifestyle of prayer by often withdrawing Himself to pray alone in the wilderness: "And in the morning, rising up a great while before day, he went out and departed into a solitary place, and there prayed" (Mark 1:35).

CHAPTER 9

Hearing the Humble

Coming to Jesus Weeping

"And from thence, he arose, and went into the borders of Tyre and Sidon, and entered into a house, and would have no man know it: but he could not be hid. For a certain woman, whose young daughter had an unclean spirit, heard of him, and came and fell at his feet. The woman was a Greek, a Syrophenician by nation; and she besought him that he would cast forth the devil out of her daughter" (Mark 7:24-26). His ministry grew and multitudes of people with sickness and disease sought Jesus – many believing that if they could touch him, they would be healed. Seeking respite from the toiling demands on His ministry, Jesus journeyed the north and then west to the Syrophenician cities of Tyre and Sidon. These two cities were situated on the Mediterranean Sea's shores, about 100 to 120 miles from Jerusalem. Except for His brief stay in Egypt when He was a child – this is the only record that Jesus ever traveled beyond the confines of His native Judea of Galilee. He desperately needed to find a place where He could refresh Himself physically and mentally away from the demands of His growing popularity. However, when He arrived on the Syrian coast, the disciples found that His reputation had already preceded them. They were unable to conceal Him from those who earnestly sought His ministry. Many people with needs came to Jesus, for in Him, they found love and compassion. Those who were distressed came that they might find peace and joy in His presence. It is no wonder that Jesus could not be hidden, for He, who was the light of the world, possessed power and presence that radiated and illuminated His world like a shining light that set upon a hill.

There were brokenhearted souls in Israel; nevertheless, God knew that there was a Gentile woman on the coasts of Tyre and Sidon who needed a miracle. Although this woman was an idolater and outside Abraham's inheritance, God recognized in her a humble spirit full of faith. Being a Gentile, she was not among God's covenant people. As the covenant people of God, Israel was privileged to be the custodians of God's Word and the recipients of God's favor. However, despite these blessings and privileges, Jesus never commanded the Jews of His generation for their great faith. There are only two instances in the New Testament where Jesus commended anyone for their great faith, and both of these examples involved Gentiles. The first example was that of a Roman centurion who humbly sought the Lord to speak only the word that his servant might be healed because he felt unworthy for Jesus to visit his home. To those who followed Him, Jesus said, "Very I say unto you, I have not found so great faith, no not in Israel" (Matthew 8:10). The only other instance when Jesus commended someone for having great faith was about this Syrophenician woman. To this humble outcast, Jesus spoke, "O woman, great is thy faith: be it unto thee even as thou wilt" (Matthew 15:28).

Broken and heavyhearted – this woman of Syrophenicia was weeping as she came to see Jesus. Coming to the door of the house where he was, she cried aloud in excellent travail concerning her daughter, who was deeply vexed with a demon; she sought for Jesus to heal her. In her distress, she fell at His feet and worshiped Him. She was consumed with a passion for having Jesus grant her petition. Her faith and desire to see her daughter healed so great that she did not consider the obstacles in her way. In coming to Jesus, the woman did not ask for something for herself, but she came desiring only that her daughter might be delivered of an unclean spirit. Selfishness robs a person of his ability to touch Jesus and move Him to act on his behalf. Instead, we should humbly seek first that which profits others. "Ye ask, and receive not, because ye ask amiss, that ye may consume it upon your lust" James 4:3). In every instance that God commended individuals for having great faith, He did so in response to an attitude of great humility. The Roman centurion was concerned about the health and wellness of his servant. Likewise, a Syrophenician woman considered not her own needs or extremities but was thinking only of her daughter's need for deliverance.

When we are broken and heavyhearted, we can find peace and comfort at the feet of Jesus. He was manifest in the flesh to bear our iniquities; also, he took our shame and carried our sorrows that we might be comforted through His Holy Spirit. He is sensitive and responsive to our feeling of infirmity and temptation (Hebrews 4:15-16). In her brokenness and desperation, the Syrophenician woman boldly approached Jesus – falling prostrate at His feet. By forgetting the contempt that most Jews had toward Gentiles, she humbly knelt at His feet and sought that He grant her petition. At the feet of Jesus, people found grace and mercy – the lame, blind, mute, maimed, afflicted, and tormented, all found miraculous deliverance. For whatever cause, the ungodliness, paganism, and idolatry of Tyre and Sidon, it allowed the child of the Syrophenician woman to become a victim of demonic possession. It seems almost inconceivable that such a young child could be possessed of an unclean spirit, yet the Bible says she was grievously vexed with a devil (Matthew 15:22). Satan has not relinquished his assault on the youth of the twenty-first century. Just as he victimized the young people of Jesus' day, he bombards our young people with occult, astrology, witchcraft, drugs, illicit sex, demonology, heresies, and false doctrine. Teen suicide is now one of the leading causes of death among adolescents. As depression, anger, and teen violence continue to litter our streets with hopelessness and despair, we must pray for the United States and all nations that God would deliver our children with a mighty move of the Holy Ghost.

Whenever we call on the name of the Lord, we know that He hears our prayers. However, there are times when we question whether He hears our petitions. God does not always answer our prayers immediately, but He always explains at the appropriate time. When the Syrophenician woman cried after the Lord Jesus, He answered her not a word but continued as if He had not heard. Yet she continued to implore Him despite the angry objections of His disciples. We also must keep faithfully calling on the name of Jesus if we are to receive an answer to our prayers. Jesus said, "Ask, and it shall be given you; seek, and ye shall find; knock, and it shall be opened unto you: for every one that asketh receiveth; and he that seeketh findeth, and to him that knocketh it shall be opened" (Matthew 7:7-8). God requires persistence and constancy in prayer, which often tests our faith. God tried the faith of this Gentile woman by testing her endurance and determination. Although she was part of a pagan culture despised by the Jews, she would not be denied her petition. As a result, she would discover that even a Gentile could receive mercy by approaching the Lord in sincere humility.

Coming to Jesus Worshiping

In the heart of every born-again believer resides an intense desire to worship God. A love for God and His house springs up from within the soul of everyone who has tasted of the precious fruit of salvation. Such worship is spontaneous and joyful without pretense or forced compliance. These types of worshippers are filled with the Holy Ghost and are baptized with the joy of the Lord. "For the kingdom of God is not meat and drink, but righteousness, and peace, and joy in the Holy Ghost" (Romans 14:17). The Syrophenician woman knew not the saving grace of the Lord Jesus Christ or His healing power; nevertheless, she did not have to be told to worship the Lord. Her worship was passionate and sincere, needing no encouragement – for she was thoroughly convinced that Jesus would free her daughter from her torment. Her desperate cries for mercy were augmented by her faith that Jesus was indeed the Messiah, Son of David: "And, behold, a woman of Canaan came out of the same coasts, and cried unto him, saying, have mercy on me, O Lord, thou son of David; my daughter is grievously vexed with a devil" (Matthew 15:22). Despite the silence of Jesus, she continued worshiping, lest she is denied her petition. Through her persistence in worship, she gained the attention of Jesus and, ultimately, the miracle for which she diligently sought.

The disciples of Jesus misunderstood His silence as an indication that He was unconcerned with this poor Gentile woman's need. Although we may judge them harshly for their apparent insensitivity and seeming prejudice, we often are disposed to think that if God does not answer our petitions swiftly, it is because our requests are not worthy of His attention. Such misjudgment on our part keeps us from participating in the blessing of the Lord. Likewise, the disciples of Jesus misunderstood His silence and urged Him to send her away – being disturbed by her continual worship and petition. They desired to send her away because she distracted them from their selfish agendas and shamed them by her faith that Jesus was the Son of David. As Christian, we should never become so wrapped up in our self-interests and involvement that our actions or attitudes send away those who seek truth and salvation. The disciples tried to send the woman away – they failed. She had come worshiping in faith, and she would not be denied (Eivaz 2016, 31)[25]. In humility, she continued to cry out to Jesus, not allowing her sensitivities to be offended.

As the Messiah of Israel, Jesus Christ's primary mission was to turn the Jewish people's hearts back to God. The Jews were God's chosen people to be a witness unto all nations. Therefore, God planned that Israel should share the good news of the gospel with the Gentiles. At the time of Jesus' visit to Tyre and Sidon, Israel had not yet recognized Jesus as the Messiah. Therefore, His primary mission was still unfinished regarding the spiritual restoration of the Jews. For this reason, Jesus answered the Syrophenician woman saying, "I am not sent but unto the lost sheep of the house of Israel" (Matthew 15:24). He reminded her that He was a Jew and that His mission was first to the Jewish people. Moreover, the custom prevented Jews and Gentiles from socializing together. Despite Jesus's apparent reluctance to honor her petition, she continued to worship Him. If His answer to her plea sorely tested her, it was not evident as she persisted in her request. Yet He was only testing the sincerity of her faith – His reply was, "It is not meet to take the children's bread and to cast it to dogs" (Matthew 15:26). She immediately understood the implication that she, being a Gentile, was considered unworthy of God's blessings by the Jews of that day. Jesus using the phrase "dog" was not to degrade her but to contrast the attitude of the Jews against His own. Furthermore, the Greek word Jesus used could be translated as "little puppy." Nevertheless, she did not take offense at His choice of words but acknowledged that though she might be considered a dog by others - she could still receive the blessing of God. Her reply reveals her remarkable faith and humility: "Truth, Lord: yet the dogs eat of the crumbs which fall from their masters' table" (Matthew 15:27).

---

[25] Jennifer Eivaz. *The Intercessors Handbook: How to Pray with Boldness, Authority, and Supernatural Power.* Minneapolis, Minnesota. Chosen Books: Baker Publishing Group. 2016. Pg. 31

Coming to Jesus Humbly

God does not always answer our prayers immediately – but He always responds. As many Christians have observed, "Sometimes the answer is "No," and sometimes the answer is "Yes." Moreover, sometimes His answer is, "Wait." Although God desires to meet our needs, He knows that to challenge and strengthen our faith divine delays are occasionally necessary. As Christians, we must not allow delays to weaken our faith or disappoint us. David wrote, "Rest in the Lord, and wait patiently for him" (Psalm 37:7). When we become anxious and doubt, it weakens our faith because we fail to rely on the promises of God. On the other hand, many are disappointed in their answer from God because they ask amiss. On the contrary, the Syrophenician woman placed her faith in the loving compassion of God – being a stranger to the promises of God. Therefore, by her faith, the Scripture was fulfilled: "All nations whom thou hast made shall come and worship before thee, O Lord; and shall glorify thy name" (Psalm 86:9). The Syrophenician woman refused to be disappointed by Christ's silence or the offending of her pride because she had a need that she earnestly desired for Jesus to meet.

What could have ended in a bitter disappointment resulted in the Syrophoenician's woman daughter's healing because of her humble spirit and unwavering faith. God honored the faith and humble spirit of this Gentile woman. God is just, and He will not cast us aside when we approach Him with the right attitude. The prophet Isaiah declares:

> "He giveth power to the faint; and to them that have no might he increaseth strength. Even the youths shall faint and be weary, and the young men shall utterly fall: but they that wait upon the Lord shall renew their strength; they shall mount up with wings as eagles; they shall run, and not be weary, and they shall walk, and not faint" (Isaiah 40:29-31)

There is an excellent reward to those who trust in the Lord. Jesus promised the church, "And whatsoever ye shall ask in my name, that will I do, that the Father may be glorified in the Son. If ye shall ask any thing in my name, I will do it" (John 14:13-14).

God honors those who live humbly, but God resists the proud and arrogant. Pride prevents us from recognizing our dependence upon God. Only when we realize our weakness and our unworthiness of the blessings of God – then are we able to receive His grace and strength. The Word of God states:

"Trust in the Lord with all thine heart, and lean not unto thine own understanding. In all thy ways acknowledge him, and he shall direct thy paths. Be not wise in thine own eyes: fear the Lord, and depart from evil. It shall be health to thy navel, and marrow to thy bones" (Proverbs 3:5-8).

Throughout the Bible, in many instances, all the wisdom of man is but a drop in a bucket compared to the vast ocean of God's wisdom and understanding. He regards not man's person or men high degree, but He searches for the meek and lowly of heart: "For thus saith the high and lofty One that inhabiteth eternity, whose name is Holy; I dwell in the high and holy place, with him also that is of a contrite and humble spirit, to revive the spirit of the humble, and to revive the heart of the contrite ones" (Isaiah 57:15).

Coming to Jesus

Sometimes sickness, tragedy, or adverse circumstances must befall individuals for them to recognize their helplessness and dependency upon God. As long as everything goes well, people tend to forget the source of their blessings. Israel's people failed God when they had a self-sufficient attitude and did not give glory and honor to God. However, in times of distress, Israel always called on God for deliverance. On today, April 9, 2020, in the United States, the coronavirus death toll jumped to over 16,679, according to Johns Hopkins University, with more than 468,703 confirmed cases. According to Governor Andrew Cuomo, New York recorded its single-day record for COVID-19 deaths, with 799. Even though the churches are closed, and most of all the religious activities are at a halt, many unsaved individuals ask for prayer, seek information about the end-time events, and ask about God in General. In this global pandemic and crisis, people are more focused on the Lord God Almighty. Desperation compelled the Syrophenician woman to seek deliverance from Jesus for her daughter. Nothing could stand between her and her great faith in the power of God through Jesus Christ to set her daughter free. The miracle of her daughter's deliverance was made possible because of her excessive burden and profound sorrow. This deep sorrow, as tragic as it was, was the incentive for bringing her to the feet of Jesus Christ. Sometimes we, too, experience pain and sadness in our lives. Yet if that sorrow causes us to turn to the Lord in faith, its price is far higher than fine gold.

The grace of Jesus Christ broke down the barrier that separated Jews and Gentiles from the promises of God. Jesus came into the world to redeem the lost - both Jew and Gentile. "For I am not ashamed of the gospel of Christ: for it is the power of God unto salvation to everyone that believeth; to the Jew first, and also to the Greek" (Romans 1:16). Although she was a Gentile, the Syrophenician woman recognized the power of God in Jesus Christ. Her faith appropriated the miracle of healing that many of the Jews had refused through unbelief. Therefore, the children's bread became a source of strength to a Gentile woman and her daughter. She had asked for nothing more than crumbs, but she received the full loaf of God's miraculous power and strength. The harvest's first-fruits are the golden heads of grain or early ripened fruit of the impending harvest. They are a token or emblem of the much higher anticipated yield. The Syrophenician woman received the Lord Jesus Christ, a measure of His glorious kingdom established in every true believer's hearts and minds. As a Gentile, her blessing was a type of first-fruits to all Gentiles who should believe in the Lord Jesus. Having asked for but a "crumb," her reward amazes us in that her daughter received complete healing and deliverance. If this healing and deliverance from God are but a "crumb," how much more productive and comprehensive of blessings await us at the table of the Lord! Indeed, the psalmist David wrote, "Thou preparest a table before me in the presence of mine enemies: thou anointest my head with oil; my cup runneth over" (Psalm 23:5).

CHAPTER 10

Establishing Priorities

First Priority – Prayer

"I exhort therefore, that, first of all, supplications, prayers, intercessions, and giving of thanks, be made for all men; for kings, and for all that are in authority; that we may lead a quiet and peaceable life in all godliness and honesty. For this is good and acceptable in the sight of God and our Savior; who will have all men to be saved, and come unto the knowledge of the truth" (I Timothy 2:1-4).

The preeminence of prayer in a believer's life is seen by the words "first of all" in verse 1. Apostle Paul recognized that life is full of many demands – making a living, raising a family, caring for a home, and only functioning in society involves a considerable commitment of time, energy, and resources. The exact nature of these activities can quickly crowd out the more vital pursuits to which the Spirit calls us. To ensure a balance of our time, Paul calls us to actively and purposefully place prayer "first of all" in our lives. Prayer should be a significant item on our list that we must put on our schedule first. Prayer should be first in our lives in at least two ways. First, in importance – prayer should be our priority. Only when prayer is our priority will we find time to pray, a place to pray, and the words to pray. Prayer is not just an obligation; it is an opportunity. The proper perspective should not be that we have to pray but that we get the excellent opportunity to pray. It is incredible and miraculous that a sovereign King of kings would listen to a human being's words. The same One who keeps the stars in place and planets in orbit hears every word that is whispered in prayer. God is moved by every cry of the parents of a sick child. He responds when the contemptible of sinners awkwardly expresses his remorse. To have such an audience with God, we must make prayer the first of our importance.

Secondly, prayer must be the first in order of action – the right attitude toward prayer causes us to place it first in our lives. Too often, prayer comes as a reaction to circumstances in our lives or as a last resort after other efforts fail, but that is not God's will. Instead, the Lord calls us to place prayer first in our lives. We should pray for direction before we make decisions. We should pray for protection before we begin trips. We should pray for health and financial provision before crises of sickness or financial problems arise. One might wonder how many dilemmas we could avoid if we took adequate time to place prayer first in our lives and allowed God to work miracles of which we might even remain unaware. The psalmist's words echo with truth: "Early will I seek thee" (Psalm 63:1). When adequately viewed and valued, we will include prayer in our daily lives. We will place it ahead of other less essential desires, even at the expense of physical comfort. While the specific time for prayer may vary from person to person, each sincere person will place prayer first in their day's actions.

In I Timothy 2:1, Paul dealt with the priority of prayer and also the content of prayers. Prayer is a mosaic made up of many facets. While this verse is not exhaustive – it does list four specific aspects that each person's prayer life should include. The first element of prayer mentioned is supplication. This element is perhaps the most common and first learned point of speaking to God, which encompasses our requests and desires to Him. God indeed desires to be more to us than only the recipient of our daily "wish list," but it is also is true that He wants us to bring Him our needs. Indeed, Paul instructed the Christians at Philippi: "Be careful about nothing, but in everything by prayer and supplication with thanksgiving, let your request be made known unto God" (Philippians 4:6). The second element is prayers. While the English word "prayer" seems to be a generic reference to prayer, the Greek word translated here is proseuche; proseucha – a prayer addressed to God. It carries with it a strong emphasis on worship. A portion of our prayer should acknowledge and appropriately honor God. This refers less to exuberant praise than it does to humbly bowing before Him. This is the portion of our prayer in which we ask what we can do for God rather than asking God to do things for us. Either facet without the other is unbalanced and leads to ineffective praying.

The third element is intercession. Intercession is that portion of our prayer when the Holy Ghost uses us to make a difference for others. Intercession is a delightful and powerful extension of Christ's ministry on earth. The Scriptures say, "Wherefore he is able also to save them to the uttermost that come unto God by him, seeing he ever liveth to make intercession for them" (Hebrews 7:25). Intercession has been linked to standing between someone and a dangerous circumstance and allowing our prayers to affect the outcome positively. It is exhausting and often draining work to take upon oneself the agony of another and pray for him or her with all fervency as if he was praying for himself. But God has called us to carry this type of burden. The last element is giving thanks. A lack of gratitude in a person is considered as an appalling attribute: "Because that, when they knew God, they glorified him not as God, neither were thankful, but became vain in their imagination, and their foolish heart was darkened" (Romans 1:21). If any born-again person only pauses to notice the blessings that have been abundantly showered on him, he will find sufficient cause to spend time offering prayers of giving thanks to the Lord.

The final aspect of the instructions regarding prayer in this verse involves the admonition that prayer is to be made "for all men" (I Timothy 2:1). In the same manner that God had graciously given salvation to us without consideration for our worthiness to receive it, so also are believers called to pray for people of all walks of life without prejudice. Indeed, we are to pray for other believers. The mutual support and concern on which the family of God is built remain on the great blessing of belonging to the body of Christ (Olson 2016, 19, 39)[26]. The Scriptures call us to "bear ye one another burdens, and so fulfill the law of Christ" (Galatians 6;2). We also are to pray for sinners. The church's primary mission is to carry on the work of Christ in seeking the lost. Prayer is vital to that effort, for without it our compassion would quickly diminish in the face of conduct so contrary to the ways of our Lord.

When we take on ourselves the burdens of prayer for a lost neighbor, love one, or co-worker, we are taking the first step toward fulfilling the

---

[26] Robert E. Olson. *The Mosaic of Christian Belief: Twenty Centuries of Unity and Diversity*. Downer Grove, Il. InterVarsity Press. 2016. Pg. 19, 39.

mission given to us by Jesus Christ. Lastly, we are explicitly called in this passage to pray for governmental leaders: "For kings, and for all that are in authority" (I Timothy 2:2). This is perhaps less difficult to do today than for Timothy and those he shared this letter. Those of us who enjoy political freedom often take our governmental leaders for granted. It is difficult for us to imagine the anxiety this commandment to pray for those in authority would have had in a society under Roman oppression. The writing of apostle Paul in I Timothy closely corresponds with the church's persecution by Emperor Nero in A. D. 65. In the face of cruelty and unjust oppression, Paul told the church that their proper response was to pray for Nero – not that God would punish him, but that God would save him! This would lead to the church having the freedom to "lead a quiet and peaceable life in all godliness and honesty" (I Timothy 2:2).

Priorities for All

The priority that every person should have is the salvation of his soul. Undoubtedly, nothing surpasses this for importance! The Lord certainly desires for all humanity to be saved (I Timothy 2:4). Salvation is more important than treasure. In the secular age in which we live, the almighty dollar has become the focal point of far too many people. In general, the accumulation of wealth is the primary indicator of success in life. This philosophy stands in stark contrast to the words of our Lord in Mark 8:36-37, "For what shall it profit a man, if he shall gain the whole world, and lose his soul or what shall a man give in exchange for his soul?" Those who invest every possible hour into accumulating material goods fail to realize the truth that: "where your treasure is, there will your heart be also" (Matthew 6:21).

Salvation is more critical than pleasure. Another hard ensnare of our age is a self-gratifying pleasure. This is true both of the activities that are transgressions against God and those merely for amusements. Whether a given interest is blatantly sinful or not, all too often, it caters more to the flesh than to the Spirit. We would do well if we realize that the New Testament salvation experience remains the most pleasurable moment in life. Nothing that man has ever created can compare to the joy of a moment spent in God's presence! Salvation is more important than life.

It is unfortunate that only toward the close of a person's life can he or she grasp the significance of the wise words of James: "For what is your life? It is even a vapor, that appeareth for a little time, and then vanisheth away" (James 4:14). In our youth, it is difficult to realize how brief seventy years can be. It seems to stretch before us like an endless road, but the destination draws close with mind-blowing speed. Consequently, each person's decision regarding his eternal salvation is far more critical than anything about this life. Salvation is an important priority for all humanity.

It is crucial to separate knowledge of the truth from salvation; the two are adamantly linked. However, the apostle Paul also listed this attribute as one of the Lord's desires for us: "Who will have all men to be saved, and come unto the knowledge of the truth" (I Timothy 2:4). Perhaps the intended emphasis is that of all the knowledge man might accumulate – no parentage of knowledge surpasses this knowledge. In other words, knowledge of the truth should be another top priority for all people. In general, man's knowledge has increased more in the last fifty years than in all the rest of the recorded history combined. The relatively recent startling advance in technology would render the world unrecognizable to those deceased only a generation ago. Yet the earth peoples have only proven the accuracy of the Scripture that describes them: "Ever learning, and never able to come to the knowledge of the truth" (II Timothy 3:7). Knowledge of the truth does not come accidentally to individuals. Instead, gaining this most precious wisdom can only happen through a sovereign work of the Holy Spirit. This knowledge is too superior for man to attain on his own; It comes by the illumination of the Holy Spirit: "But the natural man receiveth, not the things of the Spirit of God: for they are foolishness unto him: neither can he know them, because they are spiritually discerned" (I Corinthians 2:14).

Immediately after articulating God's desire that men would know the truth, Paul expressed one of the foundational truths that every man should understand – the knowledge of who God is and the singular nature of His person: "For there is one God, and one mediator between God and man, the man Christ Jesus" (I Timothy 2:5). Throughout the centuries, the devil has done all he can to introduce confusion in the simple concepts – that God is one. "Hear O Israel: The Lord, our God, is one Lord" (Deuteronomy 6:4). Therefore, this foundation of true Christianity is essential to attaining the knowledge of God. Additionally, anyone who would know God must realize and comprehend the man Jesus Christ's role as the one mediator between God and men. The dictionary defines a mediator a "one who negotiates between contending parties with a goal of reconciliation." That is what Jesus did as our mediator! In His deity, He brought God to man, and ins His humanity, He brought the man to God.

The man Christ Jesus stepped between the righteous judgment of a Holy God and the accumulated sins of lost humanity to reconcile the world unto Himself: "To wit, that God was in Christ, reconciling the world unto himself, not imputing their trespasses unto them; and hath committed unto us the word of reconciliation" (II Corinthians 5:19). This act was accomplished by Jesus becoming the substitute for our sins at Calvary. "Who gave himself a ransom for all, to be testified in due time" (I Timothy 2:6). Finally, there was something about really knowing God in the fullness of His identity that enabled a person to worship God in holiness genuinely. Perhaps that has to do with the fact that any similitude of righteousness we may have originates from Him. Paul brought his thoughts on prayer and the knowledge of God together in verse eight as he wrote about prayer and "lifting up holy hands." "I will therefore that men pray everywhere, lifting up holy hands, without wrath and doubting" (I Timothy 2:8).

A Priority for Women

The balance of Paul's remarks in I Timothy 2 relates specifically to some of the priorities that he applied to the ladies. However, we should recognize that the fundamental principles to which Paul appealed use also to men. The Lord's purpose in anointing Paul to write these words had nothing to do with impeding women unjustly with needless rules and regulations. Instead, God was pointing out their privileged position as primary mirrors of His holiness to this world. All Christians are to be holy because God is holy. However, it is apparent from this passage that the sanctified ladies are to be a focal point of displaying the work of the Holy Ghost in our lives: "I will therefor that men pray everywhere, lifting up holy hands, without wrath and doubting. In like manner also, that women adorn themselves in modest apparel, with shamefacedness and sobriety;

not with broided hair, or gold, or pearls, or costly array" (I Timothy 2:8-9). Uniquely, this is an important position to fill! The priority for a Christ lady's conduct listed in this passage is that she be modestly adorned. God wants His Holy character to live out in Godly ladies' lives to manifest to the world a sincere desire to be decent.

Moreover, a modestly dressed lady stands in stark contrast to the Spirit of this age, testifies by her outward appearance, and a witness to the One she serves. When speaking of a modest dress, our clothes should adequately cover our bodies. With the fall in the garden, Adam and Eve lost the covering of God's glory and a need for the first time to have clothing to cover their nakedness. This has been God's plan ever since. The devil has fought against this truth throughout time, as evidence in many ways. For example, in Luke 8:26-35, the demoniac in Gadara was unclothed when under the devil's grip, but once the Lord delivered him, he was clothed and in his right mind at the feet of Jesus. The beauty of a Christian lady is not in an extravagant display of wealth or the latest styles. Instead, it is a meek and quiet spirit that manifests the Lord's work of salvation and holiness in her life.

All of life is about making the right choices. This is true for the priority that a lady sets in her life. If she desires to serve the Lord and please Him – she will make proper choices. If, instead, she wants to live first unto herself, she will make different choices. However, the blessings of God go along with the direct proportion to our willingness and wisdom to make the right decisions. According to the Scriptures, there are things to avoid. Paul specifically addressed some items that do not reflect well on a Christian lady's, and therefore she should avoid them. "Not with broided hair, or gold, or pearls, or costly array" (I Timothy 2:9). The vain display of wealth in our appearance does not speak well of the stewardship to which God has called us. It demonstrates pride, which the Lord hates! The "braided hair" referenced in I Timothy 2:9 (or "plaited hair" in I Peter 3:3) referred to the cultural practice of that day of creating bizarre hairstyles that included the weaving of golden thread and pearls into the hair. Such obvious calls for attention are not in keeping with the meek and humility and Spirit of our Savior, which should be manifest in us all.

In the same measure that godly women avoid certain activities, items of apparel or adornment, and attitudes that do not please Christ, she also seeks to add to her life those things that delight Him. The Godly woman is called to add good works to her life: "But (which becometh women professing godliness) with good works" (I Timothy 2:10). These are not works to obtain salvation because this passage, like all those in the epistles, was written to those who already were converted. Instead, this was a call for ladies to seek to fulfill a virtuous woman's characteristics, as found in Proverbs 31. A lady should be diligent about her duties to her home, her spouse, and her children. By so doing, she further leaves an excellent witness to those who observe her.

CHAPTER 11

The Teaching of Jesus About Prayer

The Simplicity of Prayer

"But when ye pray, use not vain repetitions, as the heathen do: for they think that they shall be heard for their much speaking. Be not ye, therefore, like unto them: for your Father knoweth what things have ye need of before ye ask him" (Matthew 6:7-8). Prayer is a simple activity, nevertheless a powerful one. To pray is to talk to God, to call on Him, to cry unto Him, to confess to Him, to bring our requests unto Him, and to give thanks to Him for all He has done. Prayer is the spirit of the man communicating with the Spirit of God. It is the mind of a man seeking oneness with the intention of God. Luke 18:1 states, "men ought always to pray and not faint." Granted, a person may pray silently, softly, or loudly. He may pray weeping or rejoicing; he may kneel, stand, sit, lie, walk, run, or ride as he prays. The circumstances and the reason for praying may determine how he prays, but prayer is God's idea, and He has established definite principles that make prayer effective. If a person is without knowledge of these principles, he may pray without results and conclude that God does not answer prayer. Perhaps this is the reason why some people have never had a meaningful prayer life.

In simple words, Jesus taught men how to pray and how to receive answers to prayer. We are to ask God, believe that He will answer, importunity if necessary, wait on Him, and receive from Him. Moreover, Jesus taught that we should pray in His name: "And whatsoever ye shall ask in my name, that will I do, that the Father may be glorified in the Son. If ye shall ask anything in my name, I will do it" (John 14:13-14), and therein lies the authority for asking in prayer. There are scriptural qualifications for whose prayers God will answer. The apostle Peter wrote, "The eyes of the Lord are over the righteous, and his ears are open unto their prayers"

(I Peter 3:12). John also mentions some qualified requirements of prayer in his first epistle: "And whatsoever we ask, we receive of him, because we keep his commandment, and do those things that are pleasing in his sight" (I John 3:22). When we pray, we make incredible power available, energetic in its working, causing changes in our favor. The Lord specially designs specific prayer sessions to help straighten out things in the spiritual-realm regarding our immediate or later future as individuals, families, or our ministries. How wonderful that we can change circumstances and alter consequences in His Name through the power of prayer (Oyakhilome 2004, 7)[27]. Every believer must spend time in prayer - for a victorious living requires it. Moreover, prayer should precede every critical decision, for we must seek God's will and carry it out. Every aspect of God's work in the church depends on prayer.

Using a word or sentence over and over in prayer is repetition. A person may repeat a word or phrase fervently for a long time and feel that he has prayed, but Jesus said the heathen do this and "think that they shall be heard for their much speaking." The number of times a person repeats a thing unto God is not the reason He answers prayer. Faith is the reason God answers prayer. There is a distinction between vain repletion and importunity. While God does not respond to a verbal marathon, He does respond to persistent prayer when that persistence is an embodiment of faith. Jesus said, "Ask, and it shall be given you; seek, and ye shall find; knock, and it shall be opened unto you" (Luke 11:9). It is proper to take the same request unto God every day until He answers. This is not vain repetition; it is importunity. When Jesus Prayed in the Garden of Gethsemane before His crucifixion, He prayed three times, "O my Father, if it be possible, let this cup pass from me: nevertheless, not as I will, but as thou wilt" (Matthew 26:36-44). Jesus' prayer was not one of vain repetition; instead, it was a prayer of importunity. People should be aware of the difference between repetition and vain repetition. For example, a person may cry out repeatedly in desperate need beseeching God to deliver him from his affliction. This repetition is not futile, for Jesus said in one place, "Shall not God avenge his own elect, which cries day and night unto him, though He bears long with them?" (Luke 18:7).

---

[27] Chris Oyakhilome., Ph.D. *How to Pray Effectively.* Huston, Texas. Love World Publishing Ministry. 2004. Pg. 7.

God knows everything. He knows our needs and desires. He knows what is good for us and what is not suitable for us. The psalmist David wrote, "Thou knowest my downsitting and mine uprising, thou understand my thought afar off. Thou compassest my path and my lying down, and art acquainted with all my ways" (Psalms 139:2-3). A person's prayer does not reveal to God something that He does not already know, nor does it make God more aware of the need. Many people have asked, "If God knows what we need, why doesn't He give it to us? Why do we need to ask in prayer?" Asking is praying, and God chose prayer to be the method through which He would work in a person's life. For this reason, Jesus said, "Ask, and it shall be given you" (Matthew 7:7). Everything we need is in God's hand, as the psalmist revealed: "Thou openest thine hand, and satisfies the desire of every living thing" (Psalms 145:16). But God does not back a massive truck into our driveway and unload it all at once. As a person is in need, he asks God in prayer to grant that specific need, and God supplies the need by His mercy. Because of this process, the person is continually reminded of the source of his blessings. It is God who provides for all our needs, "Nevertheless he left not himself without witness, in that he did good, and gave us rain from heaven, and fruitful seasons, filling our hearts with food and gladness" (Acts 14:17).

The Pattern for Prayer

Though a person may pray using the very words of Jesus, Jesus actually taught a manner of prayer – "After this manner therefore pray ye" (Matthew 6:9). In the first place, he was only showing a prayer pattern because He said, "After this manner therefore pray ye." We should realize that Jesus was not teaching us to pray this prayer in particular, but showing us a guideline, letting us understand that in prayer, we begin by worshipping and praising God (C. Oyakhilome 2004, 53)[28]. A person may pray in this manner and never recite the Lord's prayer. However, the words of Jesus are so profound they cannot be improved. The prayer is directed to the true God, acknowledging His name, His holiness, and His kingdom. We

---

[28] Chris Oyakhilome., Ph.D. *Praying the Right Way.* Huston, Texas. Love World Publishing Ministry. 2004. Pg. 53.

are to request that God's will be done in the earth as it is in heaven. Then the prayer is directed toward expressing our needs, both materially and spiritually, and that God would treat us as we treat others. How can we expect God to treat us well if we do not do the same to others? Finally, we pray for moral direction and deliverance from evil and acknowledging that all power and glory belong to God.

"Our Father which art in heaven" (Matthew 6:9). The prayer begins with the possessive pronoun "our." Indeed, God is our Father. This takes for granted that we are His children. To claim possession of God as our Father, we must submit to His ownership of us as His children. According to the apostle Paul, the Lord has promised, "Wherefore come out from among them, and be ye separate, saith the Lord, and touch not the unclean thing; and I will receive you, and will be a Father unto you, and ye shall be my sons and daughters, saith the Lord Almighty" (II Corinthians 6:17-18). This relationship is the result of regeneration. Peter taught that a Christian is born again by the incorruptible seed, the Word of God. Paul wrote, "For ye are all the children of God by faith in Christ Jesus. For as many of you as have been baptized into Christ have put on Christ" (Galatians 3:26-27). Without a doubt, God always will have people who honor His name. The psalmist wrote, "From the rising of the sun unto the going down of the same the Lord's name is to be praised" (Psalm 113:3). Again, in another place, the psalmist said, "He sent redemption unto his people: he hath commanded his covenant forever: holy, and reverend is his name" (Psalm 111:9). Jesus taught His disciples to honor God's name in their prayers, for in doing so, they acknowledge his holiness as well as his sovereignty.

Prayer for God's kingdom to come creates an awareness of the need to be ready for His kingdom, and as a person becomes more kingdom-minded, he is less earthly-minded. In the spiritual realm, God's kingdom is already in place. Paul taught that God has "delivered us from the power of darkness, and hath translated us into the kingdom of his dear Son" (Colossians 1:13). The kingdom of God is "righteousness, and peace, and joy in the Holy Ghost." In God's own time, however, the kingdom will manifest to a physical kingdom. Jeremiah wrote, "Behold; the days come, saith the Lord, that I will raise unto David a righteous Branch, and a King shall reign and prosper, and shall execute judgment and justice in the earth" (Jeremiah 23:5). A person usually prays to bring about his own will, which sometimes is in order, because Jesus told His disciples to pray for "what things soever ye desire." That gives the Christian an immense latitude in prayer; he may ask and receive many things. However, that range is qualified by the will of God, for John wrote, "If we ask anything according to his will, he heareth us" (I John 5:14). People cannot expect God to answer prayer in such a conflicting way with His own will. Jesus said to pray after this manner: "Thy will be done." To do so is to accept God's will over our own will, and that requires trust. What a person sees in a given situation is influenced by his own will in the matter. However, what he does not understand may involve God's will, and God sees the end of a thing from the beginning. Therefore, the Scriptures direct us to: "Trust in the Lord with all thine heart; and lean not unto thine own understanding. In all thy ways acknowledge him, and he shall direct thy paths" (Proverbs 3:5-6).

"Give us this day our daily bread" (Matthew 6:11). This verse indicates that a person should pray in the morning for whatever he will need the entire day; however, it does not mean that prayer should be offered at other times during the day. David said, "Evening, and morning, and at noon, will I pray" (Psalm 55:17). However, the morning prayer set the course for the day as one gains control, confidence, and strength to meet the challenges that face him the rest of the day. The prayer for daily bread may be taken literally by impoverished people who trust God every day for food, and it may seem unnecessary to a person who lives in a land of plenty and never misses a meal. But we should not take God's blessing for granted. Job, a wealthy man and a servant of God, in a day lost his wealth and said, "Naked came I out of my mother's womb, and naked shall I return thither: The Lord gave, and the Lord hath taken away; blessed be the name of the Lord" (Job 1:21). The bountiful supply that one enjoys today may be taken away tomorrow by a season of unemployment, long-term illness, or even the death of a person who provides for the family. When a nation suffers the devastations of a pandemic, wars, or natural disasters, food and water often become scarce. It would seem that even if a person's pantry is full, he still should pray, "Give us this day our daily bread."

We should pray for forgiveness. "And forgive us our debts, as we forgive our debtors" (Matthew 6:12). A person who sins against God becomes indebted to Him. In Luke's account of this prayer, the word "sin" is used instead of "debt." "Forgive us of our sins; for we also forgive everyone that is indebted to us" (Luke 11:4). Financial debt is not the subject here but a moral debt. Every time a person sins, he becomes more deeply indebted to God because he cannot pay for the grief that he has caused God or the damage he has done to himself. The price is infinitely beyond his means. However, when Christ taught this lesson, He knew that He would soon offer Himself: "How much more shall the blood of Christ, who through the eternal Spirit offered himself without spot to God, purge your conscience from dead works to serve the living God" (Hebrews 9:14) and obtain "redemption through his blood, even the forgiveness of sin" (Colossians 1:14). For this reason, Jesus taught us to pray for forgiveness of our sins. A person cannot expect to receive forgiveness if he does not forgive others. A person can only be right with God if he will forgive those who are not right with him. Unforgiveness not only prevents a person from being overlooked, but it also gives Satan an advantage over that person: "To whom ye forgive anything, I also forgive: for if I forgive anything, to whom I forgave it, for your sakes forgave I it in the person of Christ; Lest Satan should get an advantage of us: for we are not ignorant of his devices" (II Corinthians 2:10-11).

We should pray for deliverance. "And lead us not into temptation, but deliver us from evil" (Matthew 6:13). God's people will be tempted, but some temptation is avoidable. Jesus said, "Watch and pray, that ye enter not into temptation" (Matthew 26:41). It would seem, then, that temptation is somewhat regulated by prayer. A person who prays will have a sharper discernment of the enemy and will be more attuned to the leading of the Holy Spirit than a person who does not pray. Consequently, he will avoid some temptation that others will face – this is an excellent reason to begin the day with prayer. The word temptation presupposes there is a tempter. In the beginning, the serpent tempted Eve to eat of the tree of knowledge of good and evil. In Revelation 12:9, the serpent is identified as the devil and Satan. Eve disobeyed God and ate the fruit of the tree. Consequently, she became a sinner, and if that were not enough, she also became a temptress; she tempted Adam: "And unto Adam, he said, because thou hast hearkened unto the voice of thy wife, and hast eaten of the tree, of which I commanded thee, saying, thou shalt not eat of it: cursed is the ground for thy sake; in sorrow shalt thou eat of it all the days of thy life" (Genesis 3:17). From this event, we learn that temptation originated with Satan, but he has plenty of help. He works through people and demons to accomplish his nefarious endeavors. While the temptation is unpleasant, we should be aware that God also limits it. For the Scriptures say, "There hath no temptation taken you such as is common to man: but God is faithful, who will not suffer you to be tempted above that ye are able; but will with the temptation also make a way to escape, that ye may be able to bear it" (I Corinthians 10:13).

The Practice of Prayer

"But thou, when thou prayest, enter into thy closet, and when thou shut thy door, pray to thy Father which is in secret; and thy Father which seeth in secret shall reward thee openly. But when ye pray..." (Matthew 6:6-7). Jesu assumed people would pray, an assumption that is justified because eventually, everyone does pray. "But when ye pray," there is a manner that is acceptable to God and a way that is not. We are admonished to practice all that Jesus taught about prayer, for therein lies the power to change individual lives and others and the situations that threaten God's people's wellbeing. By all means, God wants us to be unrelenting in our prayer life. He wants us to walk with Him, talk with Him, and commune with Him continually – day after day in this age and eventually throughout eternity!

The apostle Paul instructs us to "pray without ceasing" (I Thessalonians 5:17). Again, remember Jesus' example of getting up early a great while before day to pray to the Father! For prayer was vitally important to Christ. That is why He put it first on His schedule – before anything else could interfere. Evidently, Jesus probably came back to God repeatedly as the day progressed. The book of Hebrews tells us about Christ's fervent, earnest prayers: "Who in the days of his flesh, when he had offered up prayers and supplications with strong crying and tears unto him that was able to save him from death, and was heard in that he feared" (Hebrews 5:7). In essence, let us put our hearts into our prayers. Let us be fervent. Let us be passionate as we pour our hearts to the awesome God who wants to be our heavenly Father (Meredith 2008, 14)[29].

---

[29] Roderick Meredith. *Twelve Keys to Answered Prayer*. Charlotte, NC. The Living Church of God. 2008. Pg. 14.

CHAPTER 12

Commitment to the Bible

Desiring the Word

"Forever, O LORD, thy word is settled in heaven. Thy faithfulness is unto all generations: thou hast established the earth, and it abideth. They continue this day according to thine ordinances: for all are thy servants. Unless thy law had been my delights, I should then have perished in mine affliction. I will never forget thy precepts: for with them thou hast quickened me. I am thine, save me; for I have sought thy precepts. The wicked have waited for me to destroy me: but I will consider thy testimonies. I have seen an end of all perfection: but thy commandment is exceeding broad. O how love I thy law! it is my meditation all the day" (Psalm 119:89-97).

When God moved upon Moses to write the first five books of the Bible, He told him what to write and what preventive measures to take to preserve the writing. Later, when scribes copied the manuscripts of the Scripture, each word was written and checked one character at a time. If a mistake was made, the entire copy was destroyed, and the scribe began copying again from the beginning of the document. God commanded that the copying should be precise; stern warnings were directed at any person who would add to or take away from His Word: "Ye shall not add unto the word which I command you, neither shall ye diminish ought from it, that ye may keep the commandments of the Lord your God which I command you" (Deuteronomy 4:2). Indeed, many trustworthy copies were produced by faithful scribes. These copies were read and recopied by the faithful scribes down through the centuries so that the same Word of God, which was fresh and alive to them in their day, is still new and active to us today. "The grass withereth, the flower fadeth: but the word of our God shall stand forever" (Isaiah 40:8). As Christians, we must not underestimate the immense value of God's Word, for it should lead us in every area of our lives. "Thy word is a lamp unto my feet, and a light unto my path" (Psalm 119:105).

While there are thousands upon thousands of books in our world that have great value to society, they cause people to think more honestly about themselves; however, only the Bible can truly change a person's life. When Satan tempted Jesus in the wilderness, Jesus responded by quoting the Scriptures (Matthew 4:1-11). When used with faith and sincerity, the Word of God is the most potent weapon to fight the temptations of the enemy. "Thy word have I hid in mine heart, that I might not sin against thee" (Psalm 119:11). When the Word of God is hidden in our hearts, we come to see ourselves as Christ sees us. "The Spirit itself beareth witness with our spirit, that we are the children of God: And if children, then heirs; heirs of God, and joint-heirs with Christ; if so be that we suffer with him, that we may also be glorified together" (Romans 8:16-17). Moreover, we are not easy prey for the devil when we know who we are! The Word of God not only gives us power over sin but also teaches us wisdom for handling our day-to-day cares of life. Another example of the power of the Word of God is seen by looking at the universe, which God created for us. The writer of the Book of Hebrews states, "Through faith we understand that the worlds were framed by the word of God so that things which are seen were not made of the things which do appear" (Hebrews 11:3).

Furthermore, it is the authority of that same word that God spoke in the first chapter of Genesis that keeps the universe functioning as we know it today. This will continue until God declares otherwise. "As newborn babes, desire the sincere milk of the word, that ye may grow thereby" (I Peter 2:2). A newborn baby needs its mother's milk to receive a properly balanced diet and, by this means, sustaining a precipitously growing body during the first several months of life. Similarly, a new Christian need to be spiritually nourished from the very basics of God's Word. A baby's nutrition during its first few months may determine its future growth, development, health, and ability to fight sicknesses that it may encounter in the weeks and months ahead. The baby Christian must also receive teaching from God's Word early in his or her spiritual walk, for knowing and obeying the Word of God provides an avenue for growth as well as a defense system against temptation and mental attacks from the enemy. Included in these teaching topics should be the new birth experience, the grace of God, faith, and trust in God. Moreover, the new Christian needs to learn the value of a consistent prayer life combined with reading God's Word. Without this milk of the Word, the new believer will have difficulties surviving the spiritual battles they will face in life. Once the new Christian masters this necessary spiritual diet, the young believer is ready to go on to the meat of the Word. "Therefore, leaving the principles of the doctrine of Christ, let us go on unto perfection; not laying the foundation of repentance from dead works again, and faith toward God" (Hebrews 6:1).

As a new Christian grows and becomes established in Christ, he or she begins to develop character and attitudes. As the process of growth takes place in us, God directs us to particular ministry areas by which we can teach His people. However, growth is a continual process for every Christian. "I beseech you therefore, brethren, by the mercies of God, that ye present your bodies a living sacrifice, holy, acceptable unto God, which is your reasonable service. And be not conformed to this world: but be ye transformed by the renewing of your mind, that ye may prove what is that good, and acceptable, and perfect, will of God" (Romans 12:1-2). The Bible informs us that there are strength and power in the Word of God: "For the word of God is quick, and powerful, and sharper than any two-edged sword, piercing even to the dividing asunder of the soul and spirit, and of the joints and marrow, and is a discerner of the thoughts and intents of the hearts" (Hebrews 4:12). In reality, at some point in our lives, each of us has been in a position to feel the genuineness of the Word of God in action. The experience could have happened in our quiet times with the Lord or while the Lord is using His minister to reach into our hearts while preaching His Word. Regardless of the experiences, God's Word reveals things in our lives that sometimes we are not aware exist, and God allows us to repent and find spiritual strength. If we could not see the areas of our lives which need changing - we could never grow spiritually. Our spiritual walk would eventually suffer, and we could become stagnant and even backslide. Christians should, therefore, welcome the prompting of the Lord that comes from His Word.

Learning the Word

"Study to shew thyself approved unto God, a workman that needeth not to be ashamed, rightly dividing the word of truth" (II Timothy 2:15). Our benefit of studying God's written Word is its ability to provide us with a clearer understanding of His direction for our lives. Through consistent prayer and study of the Bible, God's thoughts become our thoughts, and His will becomes our will as His Word saturates our minds and spirits. The Lord desires to use each of us to reach the needs of the lost souls surrounding us each day, as well as the needs of other members of the body of Christ. In his first epistle, Peter directs the Christians to be ready to give an answer concerning their faith: "But sanctify the Lord God in your hearts: and be ready always to give an answer to every man that asketh you a reason of the hope that is in you with meekness and fear" (I Peter 3:15). When we share with the people what the Word of God tells us about salvation, we have an undeniable foundation for introducing them to Jesus Christ. By the same token, it is essential for every Christian to hear God's Word taught and preached. There are as many different styles of preaching as there are messages preached. God uses various personalities and backgrounds and ministers to speak to His people and to meet their needs. Teaching is far more than just randomly selecting a passage of Scripture and applying its context to the audience's lives; God speaks through his vessel to minister to the believers' individual needs and draws sinners to salvation. The Scriptures state, "So then faith comes by hearing, and hearing by the word of God" (Romans 10:17).

"But be ye doers of the word, and not hearers only, deceiving your own selves" (James 1:22). Our Bible study and verbal commitment to live for God are pointless if we fail to obey God's Word. If we claim to be Christians yet resist God's attempts to bring us closer to Him, we are deceiving ourselves. To be significant on the Christian journey, Christian obedience must come from their faith in God, a sincere heart, and a desire to please God. "But God be thanked, that ye were the servants of sin, but ye have obeyed from the heart that form of doctrine which was delivered you" (Romans 6:17). Additionally, God is not looking for people who merely obey rules because they feel obligated to Him. However, God desires obedience from those with a heart that says, "Father, I love You, and I want to do what is pleasing in Your sight." It is sincere obedience that causes Christians to grow spiritually in God's kingdom, for compliance is necessary for our walk with the Lord. In other words, obedience to God can be compared with a relationship between a husband and a wife. A successful marriage is based on a commitment to each other. Once a person is married, he or she will not date other people. They have an obligation to their relationship with their spouse. When a married couple fails to follow their commitment in their marriage, they will soon separate. To be a Christian, a person must commit himself to Jesus Christ, but if he fails to live up to his commitment, he will soon drift away and lose his relationship with Christ.

Prayer is one of the Christian's highest privileges and responsibilities. However, a common hindrance to a successful prayer life is a failure to understand how God wants us to pray. In Matthew 6:7-15, Jesus taught His disciples to pray by giving them an outline to follow. We, too, can learn how to pray from this outline. This is not to mention that we should recite the simple prayer we call the Lord's Prayer. Neither does it mean that we should go out and purchase a book of prayers to recite to God. Instead, we are to spend time in Bible study to discover what the Word of God teaches us about prayer. Indeed, one feature often used in prayer is to quote verses of Scriptures because the Word of God builds faith in our hearts to believe God for answers to our needs (Geisler, Christian Apologetics 2013, 378, 788)[30]. Praying the Word of God also points us in the right direction for spiritual growth and maturity. Moreover, when we are praying the Word, we are praying God's will for our lives. As God's Word is spoken in prayer, it often becomes a true source of strength and encouragement to our souls. On a sad note, today, four months after the first case of COVID-19 was confirmed in the United States, the nation's coronavirus death toll has exceeded 100,000, as of 6 PM eastern on May 27, 2020, according to data collected by the Center for Systems Science and Engineering at Johns Hopkins University. The United States has the most confirmed deaths of any country in the world. It is comparable to the entire population of mid-sized cities like Albany, New York, or Boca Raton, Florida. More American lives were lost to the Korean War, the

---

[30] Norman L. Geisler. *Christian Apologetics*. Grand Rapids, Michigan. Baker Academic. 2013. Pg. 378, 388.

Vietnam War, and the September 11, 2001 attacks combined. Our nation is at a time and place of great mourning; nevertheless, many righteous individuals are praying during this pandemic crisis.

Spreading the Word

"I will worship toward thy holy temple, and praise thy name for thy lovingkindness and for thy truth: for thou hast magnified thy word above all thy name" (Psalm 138:2). God's Word is so important, and God is so committed to his Word that the Scripture tells us that God has magnified the Word above His name. There is no need to ponder the thought that God may decide to put aside His Word. God is committed to His Word, and He has placed within the Bible stern warning against anyone who would try to change it in any way:

> "For I testify unto every man that heareth the words of the prophecy of this book, if any man shall add unto these things, God shall add unto him the plagues that are written in this book: And if any man shall take away from the words of the book of this prophecy, God shall take away his part out of the book of life, and out of the holy city, and from the things which are written in this book" (Revelation 22:18-19

Every Christian must be committed to God's Word, for it must be alive and real to him every day. The person who commits to God's Word will find guidance, spiritual strength, encouragement, and understanding of the Word. Additionally, as the Christian walks with God, he will use the Word to reach out to people around him who need salvation. If we desire God to trust us with His kingdom's responsibilities, we must first be willing to learn and live the basics of His Word. When we commit ourselves to His Word, we will believe Him for His promises, and He will lead us into a closer relationship with Him.

"And he said unto them, go ye into all the world, and preach the gospel to every creature" (Mark 16:15). God has commissioned His people to take the gospel as recorded in His Word to the lost. If we are to share the gospel with others effectively, our commitment to the Bible must be unwavering.

For the mere fact, the Bible is the foundation upon which our faith stands. Before we can minister God's Word, we must first be students of the Word. We can only preach the Word of God to others after we have learned its message and committed our lives to live by its command, precepts, and principles. In general, Christ's body members are the channels through whom God's voice is heard in the world. We are Christ's body – His ambassadors, in this world, "Now ye are the body of Christ, and members in particular" (I Corinthians 12:27). Serving as God's hands, feet, and voice, we are to go into all the world with the good news of salvation in Jesus Christ. When we go in the power of God's Word, we will witness people receiving salvation, healing, or strength in Christ. However, our ability to share the gospel is a result of God's guidance and the anointing of the Holy Ghost. This does not disregard the value of studying the Word, for God has little to anoint if the vessel He desires to use is empty. Witnessing without the anointing of God's Holy Spirit may drive people away from the truth, but the Word with the anointing of His Spirit brings faith, conviction, and conversion.

"Go ye therefore, and teach all nation, baptizing them in the name of the Father, the Son, and the Holy Ghost: Teaching them to observe all things whatsoever I have commanded you: and lo, I am with you always, even unto the end of the world. Amen" (Matthew 28:19-20). New believers must be disciplined or taught with the Word of God. To counter the attacks on our faith in spiritual battles, we must have the sword of the Spirit. The Word of God is used both as an offensive and a defensive weapon: "And take the helmet of salvation, and the sword of the Spirit, which is the word of God" (Ephesians 6:17). By teaching the Bible to new believers, we help them defend their experience with God and overcome problems at home, work, and in the community. Moreover, having a basic understanding of God's Word will help new believers overcome personal failures, trials, and persecution. The Word increases their faith and places them on a solid foundation. In essence, the Word of God will re-educate the conscience of a person who has lived much of his or her life with no real knowledge of God. "For our rejoicing is this, the testimony of our conscience, that is simplicity and godly sincerity, not with fleshly wisdom, but by the grace of God, we have had our conversation in the world, and more abundantly to you-ward" (II Corinthians 1:12).

CONCLUSION

God requires that His people make Him first in their lives. He accepts no lower position of importance than the first place of priority. The first and most significant of all commandments is that we love God above all else and that we love Him with all our heart, soul, mind, and strength. Albeit, Christians never outgrow their need for prayer. Though some are blessed with a special ministry of prayer, all God saints need to know how to pray effectually. Jesus gave us a perfect example by which to pattern our prayer lives. He emphasized prayer both by example and by teaching. Jesus Christ commanded us to pray - He spoke of the necessity of persistent and consistent prayer. However, perhaps no other virtue demonstrates genuine Christ-likeness as much as does forgiveness. Forgiveness must be a practice among all Christians. Forgiveness typifies more about the nature of Christ than any of the power associated with the mighty acts of God, for it reveals the saving grace of our Lord Jesus Christ to lost and sinful humanity.

Prayer is one of the highest privileges for the children of God. In some instances, it is also one of the most neglected weapons in our arsenal by which we war against the flesh and the devil. Not only did Jesus preach about prayer, but He also practiced it! To be Christ-like is to be prayerful. No person is any more significant than his prayer life. Prayer is a command, and Jesus epitomized a Christian's prayer life. Prayer gives us an advantage over our enemy and increases our usefulness in the kingdom of God. Daniel exhibited the value of continued and complete dedication to God. In each part of his life, he was faithful to God. Even in the most trying circumstances, he was proven trustworthy. Being loyal to his God, he was naturally committed to his fellowman and his responsibilities. These events in his life were quite a test for youth not yet twenty years of age. As his loyalty became known in Babylon, Daniel was naturally rewarded by the authority with great position and privilege. Again, better than this commendation, God rewarded him for his devotion and diligence with divine revelation and miracles in his life.

The three vital factors – prayer, the Word of God, and the Holy

Ghost – provide an excellent foundation of stability. Prayer is that warm, intimate communion with God that nothing can replace. Through prayer, we sense the heartbeat of God. The Lord becomes our close friend to whom we can confess, praise, and petition. Daily prayer will keep the communication lines open. The Word of God is the basis of our faith. It provides the ultimate answers that guide us through life's severe problems. The Word is a stable foundation in a constantly changing world. Its principles relate to every generation, every time period, every personality type, and every social level. The Holy Ghost gives life to our prayers and our Bible reading. Our prayers are assisted by the Holy Ghost – making them a powerful force for change in our world. The Word of God is illuminated by God's Spirit, giving depth and understanding to the Christian. Walking in the Spirit assures us of a life of victory over the flesh.

In Mark chapter 5, we are told of a woman who had an issue of blood for twelve years. Having spent all her money on doctors, she heard of Jesus. Having no other hope, in desperation, she came to Jesus. The Bible tells how she purposefully pressed through the crowd that surrounded Jesus. We were reminded that although her illness made her very week, she did not give up. Her perseverance paid off. Of course, it was more than her tenacity. She had faith that if she could get to Jesus and touch His garment, she would be healed. She did, and she was healed. All her discouragements and defeats faded into extinction. She was instantly and completely healed.

Uniquely, Capernaum was generally faithless. Captivated for a time by the signs that they saw – the townspeople as a whole were unresponsive to Christ's call to repentance. Amid this lack of sympathy, however, individuals like Jairus expressed outstanding trust in the Lord Jesus. They stood out from others in that they acted decisively on their faith. People like Jairus stepped out beyond the opinion of the crowd. Despite the incredible difficulty, they entrusted their desperate needs to the Lord. The miracle that Jairus saw is evidence that it pays to trust Jesus during life's most shattering experiences. It is evidence of Christ's great concern, even during times of delay. It is proof that when others can offer no hope, there is still One who can miraculously intervene.

To help us avoid making dangerous mistakes, the Scriptures make specific, clear priorities we should establish. First, prayer should be every Christian's highest priority. We should pray for our fellow Christians, sinners, and governmental leaders. This prayer should include thanksgiving, intercession, petition, worship, and all facets that complete the foundation of communication with our Heavenly Father. Indeed, the faith of Abraham sustained him through his life. His response to the call of God was positive. The walk of Abraham through life's journey was one of obedience. The trying of his faith was more precious than gold. Though severely tested, his faith stood firm on the promises of God. There are some biblical requirements for faith to be sound.

The simplicity of prayer makes God accessible to everyone. He listens to the voice of a child earnestly as He listens to a prophet, and He hears a person who prays in his living room as quickly as one who prays in the Holy Land. Jesus taught us to pray in a specific manner, a manner in which our relationship with God is revealed and allows us to address God as our Father. As our Father, God is concerned about our needs and our desires, and as His children, we feel comfortable approaching Him. Lastly, just as our physical bodies require a balanced diet to be healthy and energetic, so must we nourish the inner man with the Word of God to be a healthy Christian. As we apply faith and make an effort to study, memorize, pray, and listen to the Word of God, our spiritual man matures and becomes stronger. In doing so, God's Word truly becomes a part of our daily lives. In essence, to know the Word of God should be one of the priorities in the presence of every Christian.

BIBLIOGRAPHY

Bosworth, F. F. "Christ The Healer." 55. Grand Rapids, Michigan: Fleming H. Revell. Baker Book House., 1993.

Cameron, Peter John, Father, O. P. "Praying with Saint Paul." In *Daily Reflection on the Letters of the Apostle Paul*, 169. Washington, DC: Magnificat Central Team, Inc., 1991.

Cardwell, Jon J. "Lord Teach Us to Pray: A Devotional Study of Christ's Model Prayer for His Disciples." 15-16. Jessup, Maryland: Vayahiy Press, 2014.

Clark, David K. "Apologetics in the New Age." In *A Christian Critique of Pantheism*, by Norman L. Geisler, 227. Eugene, Oregon: Wipf and Stock Publishers, 1990.

Cobbs, Elizabeth. "Watch and Pray." In *How to Pray Effective During the Prayer Watches*, 32. Wheaton, IL: Christ Ministries of Canton, 2018.

Conner, Kevin J. "The foundations of Christian Doctrine." In *A Practical Guide to Christian Belief*, 151-152. Portland, Oregon: City Christian Publishing, 1980.

Eivaz, Jennifer. "The Intercessors Handbook: How to Pray with Boldness." 31. Minneapolis, Minnesota: Chosen Books: Baker Publishing Group, 2016.

Erickson, Millard J. "Introducing Christian Doctrine." 274-275. Grand Rapids, Michigan: Baker Academic, 2015.

Geisler, Norman L. "Christian Apologetics." 378-388. Grand Rapids, Michigan: Baker Academic, 2013.

Kendrick, Stephen, and Alex. "The Battle Plan for Prayer: From Basic training to Targeted Strategies." 194-197. Nashville, Tennessee: B & H Publishing Group., 2015.

Ladd, George Eldon. "A Theology of the New Testament." 237. Grand Rapids, Michigan: William B. Eerdmans Publishing Company, 1993.

Lockyer, Herbert. "All the Doctrines of the Bible." 225. Grand Rapids, Michigan: Zondervan Publishing, 1964.

Lohse, Bernhard. "A Short History of Christian Doctrine." In *From the First Century to the Present*, 191. Philadelphia, PA: Fortress Press, 1985.

McWilliams, Warren. "Where is the God of Justice?" In *Bible Perspective on Suffering*, 71, 150. Peabody, Massachusetts: Hendrickson Publishers. Inc., 2006.

Meredith, Roderick. "Twelve Keys to Answered Prayer." 14. Charlotte, NC: The Living Church of God, 2008.

Olson, Roger E. "The Mosaic of Christian Belief." In *Twenty Centuries of Unity and Diversity*, 19, 39. Downer Grove, IL: InterVarsity Press, 2016.

Oyakhilome, Chris. "Praying the Right Way." 53. Huston, Texas: Love World Publishing Ministry, 2004.

Oyakhilome, Chris., PH.D. "How to Pray Effectively." 7. Huston, Texas: Love World Publishing Ministry, 2004.

Packer, J.I. "Fundamentalism and the Word of God." In *Some Evangelical Principles*, 46. Grand Rapids, Michigan: Willian B. Eerdmans Publishing Company, 1958.

Scott, Steven K. "The Greatest Words Ever Spoke." In *Everything Jesus Said about You, Your Life, and Everything Else*, 110. Colorado Springs, Colorado: Water Brook Press, 2008.

Smith, Gwendolyn. "Praying Effectively: A 7-Key Prayer Model." 65. Middletown, DE: Sheba Publication, 2016.

Spurgeon, Charles. "Spurgeon on Prayer and Spiritual Warfare." 17. New Kensington, PA: Whitaker House, 1998.

Toon, Peter. "Our Triune God: A Biblical Portrayal of the Trinity." 120. Vancouver, British Columbia: Regent College Publishing, 1996.

Tozer, A. W. "Man: The Dwelling Place of God." 92-94. Chicago, Illinois: Wing Spread Publisher, 2008.

VanGemeren, Willem. "The Progress of Redemption." In *The Story of Salvation from Creation to the New Jerusalem*, 471. Grand Rapids, Michigan: Baker Books, 2000.

VanGemeren, Willem. "The Progress of Redemption." In *The Story of Salvation from Creation to the New Jerusalem*, 277. Grand Rapids, Michigan: Baker Books, 2000.

Wagner, Peter C. "Spiritual Warfare Strategy: Confronting Spiritual powers." 125-130. Shippensburg, PA: Destiny Image Publishing, Inc., 1996.

The Bible Verses - From King James Version

ABOUT THE AUTHOR

MacArthur Edmundson was born and raised in Fremont, North Carolina, a small-town northwest of Fayetteville. After graduating from high school, he entered the U.S. Army. Mac spent 26 years on active duty and retired as a Command Sergeant Major. During his last combat tour in Iraq from December 2003 to December 2004, along with being the Battalion Command Sergeant Major, He preached the gospel along with the Battalion Chaplain each Sunday to the Engineer soldiers scattered throughout Iraq. Throughout the entire combat tour, Mac spent most of his time as a prayer warrior and intercessor. As a direct result of prayer, he has seen the hand of God move on five occasions while he was a convoy commander; encountered two wood line ambushes and three roadside bombs. In each incident, no one was hurt or harm. He is married to the formal Shirley Forte'; she is also a native of Fremont, NC. They have two children and two grandchildren. They currently reside in Fayetteville, NC. While in the military, he continued and focused on education. He is a graduate of Webster University in St. Louis, Missouri, with a Master of Art in Human Resources Development and Management. He also is a graduate of International Seminary in Plymouth, Florida, with a Doctor of Theology.

Mac Edmundson accepted the Lord Jesus as his savior in August 1982. He was ordained and licensed as a minister under J. L. Sanders Evangelistic Association in Jacksonville, Arkansas, in June 1993. He has served the Lord in different Churches/denominations and various positions such as an usher, church treasurer, deacon, Sunday School Teacher, Associate Pastor, Circuit Pastor, and Pastor for a short time while in the military at Fort Polk, Louisiana. While attending Harvest Family Church in Fayetteville, NC, and serving under Bishop and Pastor Rosa Herman, he attended the church prayer school. Afterward, he became a church prayer team member, where he actively became a prayer warrior. Mac and his family are currently members of Beauty Spot Missionary Baptist Church in Fayetteville, North Carolina, where Rev. Dr. Taijuan O. Fuller is their senior pastor. Mac is now on the ministerial team and the Assistant Chairman of the Men's Ministry. Lastly, He is presently retired from the workforce and enjoying his time as a husband, father, and grandfather.

He loves the Lord and God's people, he is saved, Spirit-filled, and he is thoroughly convinced that the Lord has called him as an Evangelist to proclaim the end-time message of our Lord and Savior Jesus Christ.